MY
STORY
FOR
HIS GLORY

To Sharon,
Blessings,
Barbara LittlePage
817-829-5930

BARBARA LITTLEPAGE

ISBN 978-1-64028-303-9 (Paperback)
ISBN 978-1-64028-304-6 (Digital)

Christian Faith Publishing, Inc.
296 Chestnut Street
Meadville, PA 16335
www.christianfaithpublishing.com

Printed in the United States of America

"No matter what your background is, you will make it
Joseph was a prisoner, yet he became prime minister
Daniel was a captive, yet he became a governor
Esther was a slave girl, yet she became a queen
God will use your story for his glory in Jesus name"

Acknowledgment

My acknowledgment to God for His love and constant presences throughout my life. I accepted Jesus when I was about five years old, but I wasn't baptized until I was nine. He never left me alone!

John 15:16

> 16 You did not choose me, but I chose you and appointed you so that you might go and bear fruit—fruit that will last—and so that whatever you ask in my name the Father will give you

Thank you all my friends and family for your love and kindness during my trials. The devil wanted to scare me and make me believe that GOD had lied to me about our church. And that GOD wanted me dead!! In May 2015 I accepted the pastor's role and I told my husband I would be a target since I took the pastors role and sure enough that is what happened. The cancer was the least of what I have been through. GOD is my master not the devil!!!! I kept remembering how Satan treated Job...just because he was a man after GOD's own heart. Well guess what? There's a woman who's after GOD'S own heart and her name is Barbara Phillips Littlepage. The LORD gave me a vision for this property and that was to build a church that would accommodate families from all over Parker County and beyond. Families with lots of babies!! I got a text just the other day that said "GOD didn't choose you because of your bank account, HE chose YOU because of YOUR FAITH". All I could say was "Praise GOD" for that because if HE took a look at my bank accounts that would be scary, and maybe HE picked the wrong pastor to build HIS vision. BUT I KNOW MY GOD and HE does not make mistakes. That's why I'm married to Glenn Littlepage and I have three great kids, Dianna, David and Matthew, plus all my wonderful grand and great grand babies. Our family is CHOSEN!!! TO GOD BE ALL THE GLORY!!!!!!!!!!!!!!!!

CHAPTER I

Unexpected Blessings

It was a warm Halloween day. The butterflies were flittering from tree to tree. The sun was glistening down through the trees as if to say God sees you and He loves you. We had been working on the foundation inside our church when my son and I decided to take a lunch break. We walked out to his truck to look at some new shirts that he had gotten.

He began to talk about life, and how things happened that he never expected to happen to him. His wife had just left him and his three sons for a man ten years her junior. David said he ask her, "When did you stop loving me?" She responded, "I never really loved you." How does someone live with someone they don't love for twenty-five and a half years? David did everything in his power to show love, to please her and provide the very best for their family.

When the separation happened, David called me and told me about it with such pain in his voice that I could barely stand to hear him speak the words. My heart was broken at the news. I had known this girl from the time she was about eleven years old.

She confessed this to David August 16th, 2016, his middle son's twenty-first birthday. That just compounded the pain. When David told me about what had happened, I remember that I had asked him to go to church with me about a month before he left for his last job.

His reply was, "Why should I go to church?" God didn't give me my job, God didn't give me my $300,000-house, God didn't give me my $100,000.00 mobile home to use on my job. *I did all that!*" I just hung my head in prayer when he told me this. I knew God would have to deal with him; I couldn't make David do anything.

All I could do was to pray, and I did. The next day, David came to my office to talk to me about what he was going through. I asked him if he would please go to church with me and his reply was, "Momma, I wouldn't be anywhere else but church now." From that day forward, David has been in church and bible study every time he had the opportunity.

About three weeks after the separation, David was still in so much pain. I wanted to do something to ease it for him. I asked him if he remembered a girl with whom he had once been engaged, named Stacy. He told me sometimes he looked at Facebook and would see her, but he hadn't thought of her lately. Then he said, "Momma can you get in touch with her?" My answer was, "I bet I can!"

I personal messaged her and asked for her phone number and told her to expect a phone call. She responded immediately and told me she was glad to hear from me and gave her number to me. I didn't tell her who would be contacting her, so she had no idea what was about to happen.

Later that evening, David texted her and asked her to call his number. She thought she was calling me. When she realized it was David, she was extremely surprised and happy to hear from him. As they talked into the night, David learned that her husband of about twelve years had left her for another woman.

She had two small children and chose not to re-marry. She learned to make her own living and not depend upon a man. She studied and became a very successful real estate broker.

This conversation lasted until the wee hours in the morning. Needless to say, David and Stacy quickly became re-acquainted and brought each other up to date on each other's lives. David told me he knew that God had kept her for him for just this time in his life.

He doesn't regret getting married to his wife because he had three handsome and well-behaved young sons. Likewise, she doesn't regret getting married for the same reason. They both are assured that God had them right where He wanted them all along.

As David and I sat talking, I couldn't help but to reflect upon my own life. A life that I tried with all my heart to make perfect in the eyes of the world. I never wanted to disappoint anyone, especially my parents.

I was born in Fort Worth, Texas to Walter Alvin and Maudina Maxine Phillips on October 19, 1945. I was Daddy's pride and joy, although not the boy he was expecting.

He called me "Bob" from then on. I loved my parents with all my heart. They took my sister Joyce and me to church every Sunday. We sat on the front row next to our parents. If we so much as made a sound, Daddy would reach around our shoulder and pinch us to remind us that he would deal with us after church.

Momma never spanked us, but told us as soon as Daddy came home from work, she would tell him and he would. I remember dreading to hear his car drive into the driveway because I knew what was about to happen. Momma would tell whatever offense we had committed and he would take his belt off and begin to beat us. Sometimes we were so bruised that we couldn't go to school.

I know they both loved us, but that was their way of discipline. Daddy had just come from WWII. He lost his only brother to that awful war, and I'm sure he was very anger at that time of his life. Momma had a hearing disability and was dealing with that. I know they did the best they knew to do.

I knew Daddy favored me in so many ways; I looked a lot like my daddy, so I tried my best to please him. If he was in a bad mood, I would never talk back to him or do anything to anger him further. On the other hand, my sister Joyce would talk back and he would take his anger out on her.

As I grew into womanhood at the age of about twelve, Daddy was the one who told me the "facts of life." For some reason, Momma couldn't do that. Daddy told me about my period and what I needed to do about it. He also said, "Never tell a boy you love him." I think he meant to say, "Don't have sex with a boy," but he couldn't say the word "sex."

I'm not sure I really understood what he meant at that age, but I did know he didn't want me to have *that* with a boy. I tried to please daddy in every way I knew.

As I grew into womanhood, I knew I was attractive to the opposite sex. I made a vow to *not* allow any boy to do what Daddy didn't want me to do.

I was in my senior year of high school when I met a very nice young man named Mike. Mike told me he noticed me over a year before he worked up courage to speak to me.

Our school was so large I didn't notice Mike until the first day of our senior year. He sat behind me in a class. The first day of class he managed to say hi to me. I thought immediately this guy is the one for me!

We began to see each other on a daily basis. Every Sunday after church, we would go to his ranch to ride horses. I always wanted a horse, but my family didn't have the means for me to have one. Mike was an only child. His father was an executive with LTV, a huge aircraft company.

Both my parents also worked there. Mike never made me feel as though I was less than he was. His parents adored me and treated me as if they loved their own child.

On my eighteenth birthday, Mike and his mother bought a beautiful lavender velvet western pant suit with a matching vest and shirt for me. At first, I didn't have boots or belt, but they made sure I had them before rodeo time.

Then for Christmas, Mike gave me a matching lavender western hat. Wow! Did I feel pampered? I never had that kind of clothes in my life. Most everything I wore Momma made at home. I always looked good in my clothes, but I still felt like they were all homemade.

When Mike's mom found out I didn't have a coat to wear to the rodeo, she loaned her best western jacket to me. I felt like I had just stepped out of a western magazine.

Mike finally asked the question that all girls wait to hear. He asked me to marry him. We started immediately planning our life together. He wanted to go to college to become an attorney.

I wasn't sure if my family could afford college, so I planned to work while Mike went to college. I knew Mike's dad would get me a good job at LTV when the time came. Our plans were pretty much set.

As soon as I could go to work through the high school program, I got a job. I worked at a department store called Grants across the street from Arlington High School.

Every evening, my mother would come to pick me up from work at 9:00 p.m., except on Saturday. I got off at six p.m.

One weekend, Mike had a church retreat he attended for the entire weekend, from Friday until Sunday afternoon. This was the first time Mike and I had been separated for any length of time.

It happened on that Friday evening, three young men came into my store and walked back to the linen department where I worked. I saw them coming so I prepared to wait on them.

They were shopping for linens for their new apartment. They were college students who were preparing to enter the spring semester at Arlington State University.

They needed towels, wash clothes, sheet sets and pillows. I gathered all the items for them except for one pillow. I had to go to the back storage room to get the extra pillow.

As I walked away, I heard my name called out, so I turned to see what they needed. Actually, they didn't need anything from me, they were commenting on how good I looked in that black dress and how pretty I was.

Two of the guys were in conversation about me, but one was staring at me. I felt uncomfortable, but flattered so I continued on my way to get the pillow for them.

That evening, when my shift was nearly over as I was about to leave, I saw one of those guys coming toward my department again. I thought he must need something else for his new apartment.

But instead, he came back to ask me out I told him that I couldn't go with him because my mother was always outside waiting on me to get off work. Also, I thought that would be a good excuse not to go with him without hurting his feelings.

He insisted that he would like to meet my mother to ask her himself. I really thought my mother would say no and that would be all there was to it. I didn't even know his name.

My mother usually asks a lot of questions before anyone could take me out, but this time she said, "If you will get her home by her curfew, she can go." He assured her, he would bring me home by 10:00 p.m.

We went to a drive-in called Pals, a popular hangout for kids to get their food and drinks. I didn't think anything else would come of it because I knew Mike would be home Sunday afternoon and I would see him again.

But what happened was this guy I called James, whose real name was Glenn, asked me out for the following evening to go to a movie. At first, I thought I shouldn't go with him because Mike and I had made a commitment, but Glenn told me the last college he attended was Southwestern Bible College in Waxahachie, Texas, so I didn't see any harm in going to a movie with him.

When he arrived the next evening, I was ready to go to the walk-in movie down town, but he had different plans. He took me to a drive-in movie instead. Almost as soon as we got settled in our parking spot, he started making advances to me. I wasn't used to being treated like that on a date.

I asked him to stop trying to kiss me, please leave me alone, but he only got more aggressive. Before I knew what happened, he had taken full advantage of me. I quickly jumped out of the car and ran to the concession stand and into the restroom crying hysterically. I never had to contend with anything like that before. After I composed myself, I went back to the car and demanded that he take me home.

The next day, his mother called and informed him that his grandfather was gravely ill and she needed him to come back home to Graham, Texas. He left without speaking to me again. His grandfather finally died in about three weeks, and then Glenn attended the funeral.

During this time, I felt so much shame and disgrace for what had happened to me I intentionally avoided seeing Mike. I wouldn't take his calls or see him at school. It only took a few days for me to realize that Glenn had gotten me pregnant. That was the one thing I vowed that I would never be, pregnant before marriage.

I immediately started to vomit at home. One day, my grandmother was visiting our house as I was throwing up in the bathroom. My sister, Joyce, made the announcement, "This is the second time Barbara has thrown up." My mother must have thought something because she made a real effort to distract my grandmother from hearing what my sister had said.

I continued to go to school, even though I was very ill every morning. I would get into my class and have to run out as fast as I got there. One time I didn't make it out in time and I threw up all over the hallway.

Also, I continued going to work every day. In about three and a half weeks, Glenn came back into the store to see me. I didn't want to see him, but I knew what he had done, and I knew I had to tell him. I told him to pick me up after work because I had something to talk to him about.

He was there at 9:00 p.m. We left to find someplace where we could talk. I told him he had made me pregnant. I was so hurt and angry at him for what had he had done to me.

I knew my future with Mike was over and I would never see him again. The pain of never being Mike's wife was unbearable to me. I didn't know how I was going to handle this. I never thought about marrying Glenn; we had only known each other for twenty-two hours when this happened.

I thought I would have to go to an unwed mother's home or have an illegal abortion. I didn't want to tell my parents for fear of hurting them or what Daddy would do for what had happened to me. I couldn't tell Mike because I knew how hurt and disappointed he would be in me, so I just avoided seeing him. The shame and disgrace were overwhelming!

After I told Glenn, he said without hesitation, "Well, we'll get married!" I didn't want to get married, especially to someone whose name I didn't even really know, but what other choice did I have?

In the '60s, nice girls didn't get pregnant outside of marriage. That very night, we went to my parents and told them that we wanted to get married and they said if we were sure, then they would give us a wedding. I was not sure, but I felt I had no other option.

My heart was broken because I never spoke to Mike again during that semester. I missed the senior prom with him, the graduation parties I knew we should be attending together. I missed our fun times together, the Sundays at the ranch, the time when I got a bad cold and Mike brought medicine for me. The time when Mike came over while I was coloring my hair, I was too shy for Mike to see me in a bathing suit top, so I put a towel around my shoulders to prevent him seeing me in a bra top. My momma took photos of us as Mike helped me with the color. I missed the visits to his house where he would play "Maria Elena" on his guitar for me. I missed his dad taking random photos of us at his home and at the ranch. I missed Mike holding my books in the hallway at school. I missed Mrs. Butler getting on our case for holding hands in the hallway for "inappropriate show of affection."

Nothing would ever be the same again! Missing Mike was the worse punishment I could have endured. Failing my parents was probably equal to the worse punishment because I knew I would only be married seven and one half months when my baby came. How could I explain that?

My parents wanted so much for me. I had disappointed them and I didn't want them to be ashamed because of something that happened to me. I blamed this all on myself for going out on Mike in the first place. At the time, I thought, well Mike is with all his church friends, what could it hurt for me to go to a movie?

CHAPTER II

Becoming Littlepage

Glenn introduced me to his mother over the phone. His parents lived in Odessa at that time. I never met his parents face to face until the evening of the wedding at Aldersgate United Methodist Church. His mother was hateful to me and mentioned that her son was being trapped.

I never told Glenn because I didn't want to have trouble between his mother and us. He asked her to bring a beautiful silver punch bowl set he bought in Mexico for her, so we could use it at our reception. She did bring it, but as soon as they got back home, she sold it. Glenn was hurt because he wanted to keep it for his children's wedding some day. He didn't understand why she did that.

Every time we were together with his parents, I tried to please her because I really wanted a good relationship with his mother. After Mike's mom was so good to me, I expected Glenn's mom to be that way also, but that never happened.

There was nothing I could do to make her like me after that. She even told me one time she wished Glenn had died when he was a young boy. She said, "That way he wouldn't have to live in this hell!" She was referring to him marrying me. And how was that hell?

Glenn and I settled into married life as well as we could. His parents paid the first month's rent for our apartment. When we first married, he didn't have a job, but soon found one with Texas Consumer Finance. He didn't make much money, but I had food and a roof over my head, and at the time that's all I needed.

Every morning, my mother would drive over to take me to school. I still had two months left. Each morning was a struggle for me because of the vomiting, but I was determined to finish my senior year. I don't know how I kept away from Mike, but I did. Although, he was constantly on my mind, I never saw him again until the following Christmas 1964.

Mike had entered the University of Texas at Austin and came home for the holidays. That evening, my daddy and Glenn decided to go deer hunting, leaving Momma, me and my new baby daughter at home. While I was feeding her, the doorbell rang. I answered it and there was Mike! My heart skipped several beats!

I was so happy to see him, but also nervous because he didn't know what had happened to me or why I quit seeing him. When he saw the baby, I'm sure he must have thought I found someone else I loved, not him! Nothing was farther from the truth, but I couldn't tell him the truth. We visited for a little while then he left. I never saw his again until our fifth year class reunion.

After graduation, Glenn and I moved to Fort Worth so he could be closer to his job. We rented a nice apartment on Locke St. from an elderly couple named Mr. and Mrs. Raines, the same street my parents lived on when they first married. That was just a coincidence, not intentional.

Actually, on the day in which I was writing this, I heard a preacher on the radio telling that there is no such word in the Hebrew language as "coincidence." Everything is a divine appointment! So, everything that happens to me is in His plan. Hmmm!

I would get up early and make breakfast for Glenn, and pack a nice lunch for him. I thought that was the thing to do because Donna Reed did that on her TV show. I was able to keep breakfast down just long enough for Glenn to leave for work, and then I would make a mad dash to the bathroom to throw up. This went on for at least the rest of the summer.

By September, we decided to move to McGregor, Texas for a higher-paying job. Glenn had a cousin and her husband who had a three-bedroom apartment. Carolyn and J.O. were kind enough to let us stay in one of the bedrooms. J.O. and Glenn worked the night shift.

That left Carolyn and me time to get into all kinds of mischief. They had an Aunt Elma who was a full-blown Pentecostal woman. You know the kind who wore long dresses and put her hair in a bun and would criticize me for wearing pants and make-up, but when I went into her bathroom, I found all kinds of make-up and fancy costume jewelry.

While in McGregor, Aunt Elma made sure we were in church every time the doors were open. Carolyn played the piano as I observed what was happening. I had never been in a Pentecostal Church. Well, except the "one" time Glenn decided to take me to "his" church after we married.

It was a Pentecostal church that he had never attended until he decided to take me there. They had a full band. At the time, I had only been in the Methodist church and all they had an organ. Needless to say, I thought we were having a party at "Glenn's" church. I had never seen people with their hands waving about and shouting Hallelujah!

One evening, Carolyn and I decided to go for a ride with Aunt Elma to look at a house for Glenn and me to rent. After looking at the house, we got back into the car. It wouldn't start Aunt Elma, a rather hefty woman, was in the back seat.

Carolyn and I decided to get out and push the car to get it started. The whole time, Aunt Elma sat in the car saying, "Girls, don't push the car; you're both pregnant." We just looked at each other, started laughing and said, "If she would get her big fat butt out of the car, it wouldn't be so heavy!"

Another way Carolyn and I occupied our evenings together was to watch TV and eat Hershey's bars that were bought for our husbands lunches. By the time we needed to prepare the lunches, there were no candies left. After all, we were eating for two!

We were in McGregor about two months when my daddy called to tell us that LTV was hiring machinists. That was a great opportunity for Glenn to learn a trade that would make us a better living.

We moved back to Arlington, Texas and into my parent's home. I was glad to be back with Momma and Daddy, because having a baby in McGregor was not a pleasant thought. It was a good two-and-a-half hour drive back to my doctor in Fort Worth.

We stayed with Momma and Daddy until our sweet baby daughter was two months old. She was born November 23, 1964. I named her Dianna Gayle because I thought that was the prettiest name I had ever heard.

I enrolled our brilliant daughter into dance class at the young age of two years. I was totally convinced that she was the smartest two-year-old in Arlington.

I found a darling house in Arlington on Marydale St. We bought the house and lived in it for ten years. Those were probably the best of times for our family. We grew to three babies. We had another child on November 15, 1968. I named him David Dale. David means the "beloved one."

He was a momma's boy. I couldn't work and leave him with a babysitter, because he cried when I would leave. The sitter called me and said, "Come get this child."

I never worked away from home after that. Our youngest was born January 26, 1973. He was named Matthew Glenn, Matthew for "God's gift" and Glenn after his father. I was really feeling the housewife-mother role I enjoyed.

I wanted our family to be perfect just like Donna Reed's family, so therefore, I did everything I knew to accomplish that. Glenn was a good provider, he went to work every day, but he lacked in family structure skills. He wouldn't take initiative when needed to defend or protect me or our family when any of his family trespassed against us.

Glenn seemed afraid to confront anyone in his family, although he had no such problem with me. I think because Glenn was the baby of his family, also called "babe," he thought they were supposed to be able to do anything to him and his family. Therefore he never defended us.

One Saturday, we visited with Glenn's brother Wayne and his wife Pat. I was about three months pregnant with our second child. We all decided to play a card game called "Crazy Eight." We were having a great time until I played a card according to the rules I had learned, which were different from Wayne's rules.

I had no idea that I was doing anything wrong until Wayne got angry and grabbed my right arm and began twisting it. He hurt me so badly that I jumped up and the chair flew backwards as he continued to twist my arm.

Glenn just sat there and did nothing. Our three-year-old, Dianna, ran into the kitchen and screamed, "Uncle Wayne, leave my mommy alone." At which, Wayne turned me loose.

I got my daughter and purse and went to the car. Glenn stayed in the house with Wayne. He left me in the car alone for at least fifteen minutes. After that time, he came out with Wayne. I suppose Glenn was trying to calm Wayne.

I had only seen Wayne a couple of times since we married, I didn't know he was volatile. Wayne didn't apologize, he did say he hoped I would come back to see him again. I never wanted to go around him again, but he was family and we did have to go around him.

Tommy was Glenn's eldest brother. He was married to June Rose. Tommy quit school in the ninth grade to marry his high school sweetheart. Tommy seemed to admire Glenn's choice of me as a wife.

One Sunday morning while we were visiting with Tommy and June, I was getting ready to go to church when Tommy came into the room where I was fixing my hair and told me I was very pretty and Glenn did good!

Tommy was always very nice to me and never made me feel like he wanted to harm me in any way. I enjoyed visiting the Tommy and June. June and I were pregnant at the same time, her third, my first. Tommy was commonly known as "Big Daddy." He was kind and helpful to everyone who needed him.

CHAPTER III

The Overseer

I was responsible for all church activities, household duties, yard work, home improvements, auto maintenance, club activities such as cub scouts, dance lessons, any discipline required, even verbal. Although, when the children were older, that would have been welcomed.

I think I was so cautious about how they were disciplined. Therefore I refused to allow Glenn to do that. I was fearful of my children being harmed. I never wanted them to miss school because of "discipline."

Church was always a very important part of our family life. We attended every time the doors were open. We had our children christened at Aldersgate United Methodist Church in Arlington, Texas.

I'm not sure I was totally aware of the importance of that ritual at the time. I just knew that it would look good if we did that for our children, and people would think well of our family.

During the time we lived in Arlington, there were several times when Glenn would use physical force to get his way with me. Mostly, over things that were minor to me, but he wanted to control the situation and would use his strength against me.

I suffered lots of pain during those episodes. I never told anyone especially my parents of any force used against me because again, I wanted everything to look perfect in my life.

I thought often of divorce, but I knew I had taken a vow before God and my parents and I didn't want to violate that vow. Also, I never wanted to have another man in my life that might harm my children in any way.

As much as I wanted to be with Mike and thought of him every day, I knew he would never harm my children. I also knew he was married; therefore, I would never ask him to leave his family for mine.

Not a day went by that Mike was not on my mind. When we had our fifteenth class reunion, I was so looking forward to it because I knew Mike would be there. The reunion was everything I hoped it would be.

Mike took every opportunity that evening to spend time talking to me, and ask about my family. I told him all the good and nothing that wasn't good.

He invited Glenn and me to come to his home for an after party with some of his friends. I was so excited to spend time with him. When we arrived, he invited us in. We soon found our seats, Glenn on one end of Mike's couch and me on the other end.

Mike excused himself and disappeared for a few moments. When he came back, he had his guitar and he sat on an ottoman in front of me. That's when he started playing "Maria Elena." That was the song he played for me all those years before at his father's house. Only Mike and I knew the reason for that song.

Glenn never knew the feelings I had for Mike, or the importance Mike was to my life. I knew Glenn never thought what he did at the drive-in caused me so much damage. He was twenty-three years old and apparently just thought it was something people did.

He never thought how he harmed me all those years ago, or how the unexplainable emotional strain I was under caused so much depression every time he would hold me down forcefully. If I didn't have his children, I wouldn't have endured that treatment.

Additionally, I was always concerned about what people would think of me if I left. What a failure my life had been. At that time, divorce was not something my family did.

As hard as I tried to get along with Glenn, I just didn't understand why he was so aggressive, rude, and disrespectful. Maybe it was because he was the baby of his family of five boys including his cousins, until baby girl cousin Caroline came along when he was about three years old.

After meeting his brothers and cousins, I'm pretty sure they roughed him up when he was little. He had dark black hair, freckles all over, and he was a little roly-poly child. His pictures reminded me of the Little Rascal Spanky.

All Glenn's family lived in Graham, Texas within walking distance of each other. I know his whole family loved him; although I'm very sure there was a lot of roughhousing with all though boys.

They spent every summer at the lake swimming. They were always racing each other and I'm pretty sure they tried their best to out swim

Glenn. He always seemed to need to win no matter what he was doing. Even when we had children, he would win against them. No matter what the game was, he won!

Glenn's manners were extremely lacking. He did things like fart on me and laugh. He thought I should see the humor in what he did, I didn't! He was thoughtless when it came to opening doors for me or helping me with other things, unless I insisted on his help. Then I would usually get a response like "My momma would do that for me."

One time just after we married, his parents came to visit us. I had cleaned the apartment so well. I wanted his mom to think I was a good wife for him. He came in from work and started undressing at the front door.

He had shoes, socks, and pants on the floor all the way to our bedroom. I begged him to pick up his things, but all he said was, "My momma will pick them up when she gets here." I was so upset that I picked everything up before they got to our apartment.

The next morning, we went to a restaurant to eat breakfast. His parents seated themselves, Glenn pulled out a chair, and I thought he was pulling it out for me. At that time, the front door bell rang out. Someone was coming in.

Glenn looked to see who was coming in as I sat in the chair. I thought he had pulled it out for me. Without looking back, he sat on my lap. I was totally embarrassed by this. He and his parents just laughed. They thought it was hilarious. What I thought was, Mike would never have done that to me.

I would be totally disgusted by the things Glenn did, but it didn't take long for me to ignore his bad manners and his rudeness. I learned to open my own doors and do other things that I needed done.

As time went on, I think we finally got into a routine that just worked for us. For the most part, Glenn and I adjusted to each other's ways. I just became Momma.

CHAPTER IV

Finding Me

After ten years of living on Marydale, Glenn told me one day that he had found a farm property in Parker County and he wanted to buy. He took me and the children to see it. I wasn't really excited about it because the old farm was just that—an old farm house and nineteen acres. Glenn told me he would fix it up and then he would build a new house within a year.

He and my daddy did fix up the old house. They turned the attic into a playroom/bedroom and built a nice staircase to it. The house turned out to be a nice three-bedroom home, but it wasn't the new house Glenn had promised. We lived in that house for about two years before I decided to take matters into my hands.

I sold some of our Textron stocks and bought twelve acres of land near Weatherford Lake. I had the septic tank and water well installed and found a house in Arlington I really loved. I contacted the builder and ask him if he could build that house on my property in Weatherford. He said, "Yes, I sure can."

He built a beautiful four-bedroom home with three bathrooms, a huge game room, and a sunken living room. My bathroom was done with chocolate toilet, sinks, tub, and had a large shower.

This was my dream home. Although, it was a beautiful home, and I loved being there, my children were all of school age and I had nothing to do during the day.

I decided I wanted to begin college classes. When I talked to Glenn about it. he just said, "No, if you need to learn anything, I will teach it to you." Because I thought of Glenn as daddy, I just accepted what he told me and went away crying.

After one year, our family was settled nicely in our new home. Glenn came into the kitchen one day and made the announcement that he had quit his job. I couldn't believe my ears. We finally got the home I thought we both wanted and he quit his job! We had retirement, paid family vacations, and a job where we were fully insured. I never had to wonder if I could take my children to the doctor! What was he thinking??

Just before he quit his job, he met a woman whose husband had just passed away. Her name was Vestie Hightower. For several weeks after he quit his job, I didn't meet this woman, so naturally I started having ideas about their relationship.

Finally, he brought her to our home. She was a large, kind, gray-haired woman who just needed a family. She was terribly lonely. She had her real estate broker's licenses and she was glad to have Glenn with her in her business.

They decided to form a company and call it Hightower-Littlepage Real Estate. Vestie was a very smart business woman, and she took very good care of Glenn.

I never had to involve myself in what he was doing at the office. He gave me enough money to manage my household. I didn't realize he wasn't learning to protect the business. It was all Vestie.

They found lots of property in Parker County and bought it as business investments. They were doing a fairly good business when the economy started slowing down.

Glenn came home one day and asked, "How much would you take for our house?" I thought if I quoted a high price, he would never be able to sell it, so I said, $100,000.00. I only had $62,000.00 in it and I thought that was a lot to ask.

The following day, he brought a doctor out to look at our house and it was gone in a week. We had about two weeks to get out! Needless to say, I was heartbroken. But, I *did* give him a price.

Vestie had a small three-bedroom house that was old and smelly, we could move into it right away. So once again, I was in a small, old house. I ended up tearing out the entire front part of the house and remodeling it. We lived in this house for about one year.

Then, after I had it looking and smelling good, Glenn called me while I was at Star Point, the boys' school, to tell me he had just sold that house. So once again, Glenn and Vestie bought another old, smelly house, and now I had to move into it.

By this time, I thought I was getting pretty good at remodeling, so I started back to remodeling again. By the time we moved into this house, it was clean and smelled good.

After about a year, a nice black lady came to my door and asked if I would sell this house to her, and I said, "Sure!" I figured if I didn't sell it, Glenn would.

So again, I found myself remodeling a house Glenn had just bought. It was a really nice three-bedroom brick house on Live Oak Lane, but it was in need of a total remodel. So off I went on another remodeling adventure. I got it finished just in time for the closing on our present house and it was ready to move into.

We lived in that house for at least ten years. I loved the house and wanted to stay there forever.

Glenn and I did pretty well until the real estate business almost came to a halt. That Christmas, Glenn hadn't had a sale in several months and our money was slim. We couldn't buy gifts for each other or our children. This was the first time we were that low.

Two days after Christmas was Vestie's birthday. Everyone in the real estate business had closed for the holidays except Vestie.

Glenn got up early and left for the office to be with her. The children and I stayed home most of the day by ourselves.

Finally, about two in the afternoon, I decided to drive to the office to see if Glenn was still there. As I pulled out our drive way, I saw him coming home. I returned back to our house and got out of the car to speak with him about taking the kids to the new subdivision and have a picnic. He refused to talk to me about it and stayed in his truck.

I became very angry at him for his lack of interest in our family picnic, so I took his key from the ignition and went back to the house. I walked in and locked the door behind me.

I thought he had his house key and he would just use it to get in. Apparently, he didn't have the house key with him. That's when I saw him turn to go to the back door with a very angry look on his face.

Glenn hadn't used force on me in a long time, but I knew his look told me what was about to happen. When he got into the house, he ran toward me and grabbed me around the neck and carried me to the bedroom and threw me on the bed. I thought if I turned my head toward the bed, he wouldn't hit my face, but what happened was he hit the back of my head so hard I started to pass out.

I decided to turn around to defend myself, and then he hit me in the left eye. The under eye was cut by a ring he was wearing. The eye became swollen, blood began squirting and it turned black immediately.

When he saw what he had done, he stopped and grabbed a wash cloth to put over my eye. I wanted to call the police, but he stopped me and promised to take me to the hospital.

We left the children at home and started off for the hospital, but when we arrived, Glenn wouldn't let me go in. He didn't want anyone to know what he had done. Weatherford was a small town; therefore, He convinced me that he would take me to the Fort Worth hospital so I said, "Okay."

However, when we got to Harris Hospital, he again would not let me get out of the car. He sped off toward Arlington and told me he would take me to that hospital, but again he did the same thing. I finally told him to take me to my parent's home, which he did.

When we got there, I met Momma coming from the backyard. She thought I had been in a car wreck. I told her that Glenn had done this to me and he wouldn't take me to the hospital. She was horrified by the sight of my face.

She told me to get into her car and she would take me to the hospital. Glenn went with us and was very ashamed at what he had done.

This was the first time there were physical signs of how he had been treating me.

The doctor put about four stitches under my left eye. I was worried that I would have a scar, but when it healed there was not even a mark. I was extremely happy about that.

This incident was what it took to make me realize that I had to do something to take care of myself. I couldn't depend upon Glenn.

Around that time, I prayed that God would give me evidence that I really loved this man. I never felt love for him all the years we had been married. How do you love someone with whom you married after only knowing such a short time?

I never thought I would take abuse like that from any man, but there I was with a black eye. That night when I went to sleep, I believe God gave me a dream, and in my dream Glenn died I quickly jumped up from the bed and onto Glenn and began kissing him all over his face and I told him, "I do love you!"

From then on, I did everything in my power to keep our marriage together; I was determined to be happy with this man that God must have sent to me.

After the stitches came out, I decided to go into Fort Worth and register at Tarrant County Junior College. When I had my student ID picture made, I had a black eye and I weighed about 150 pounds. As soon as I got into my schedule for classes, I decided I'm going to be the best student there.

The evening after I registered in college, Momma called me and asked us out to eat. I was so excited to see Momma and Daddy because I wanted to show them my student ID card.

Glenn didn't know that I had gone to register and I was almost afraid to tell him while alone. While we were eating, I pulled the card from my wallet and slid it over to Momma and said, "Look what I just did." She smiled and said, "You're in college!"

The look on Glenn's face was stunned that I would do this after he told me no. He didn't say anything to me about it at all.

I wanted to be sure I kept all my housewife duties done. Every morning, I would get up about five to start my day. I did all the family laundry, cleaned my house, fed my family breakfast, then got myself and my children ready for class by eight.

My weight dropped to 118 pounds in about a month and a half, and for the first time in seventeen years I was becoming proud of myself. I kept a 3.8 grade point average and had lots of friends at school.

Every day I would pick the boys up from Star Point School, made dinner for the family, and we ate by 4:30 p.m. After that, I would go into my bedroom and shut the door and do my studying.

Every morning when I would get ready for school, I would ask Glenn if I looked okay. Either he wouldn't answer, or he said something negative about what I was wearing. All I wanted was for him to be proud of me too.

While I was at TCJC, I was selected for the Honors Program Cluster and Phi Theta Kappa National Honor Fraternity. I was so excited. I invited Glenn, Daddy, and Momma to come for the ceremony to watch me get the award. My parents were very proud of me and I thought Glenn would be too, but he acted as though he wasn't.

After thinking about his behavior, I decided he may be worried that I would leave him since I lost so much weight and realized that I could do something without him.

That would never happen because again, I made a vow to God before I had the dream if he would show me I truly loved Glenn that I would never leave him.

The semester I was supposed to graduate, my cousin committed suicide. I had to take an accounting class to graduate. It was probably the most confusing class I had taken because I couldn't concentrate at all. All I could think of was her hanging in a closet.

I ended up dropping that course. So therefore, I couldn't graduate from Tarrant County Junior College that semester. The following semester, I enrolled at Weatherford Junior College and took the required Algebra class and graduated from there.

CHAPTER V

Broken Hearts

During 1982, we were faced with a devastating incident. Our daughter Dianna had known a young man named Brack from the fourth grade until their senior year. They had puppy love for each other for eight years.

In their senior year, Brack worked up the courage to tell me he loved Dianna with all his heart. He wanted to give Dianna a promise ring. He wanted her to be his wife someday.

He asked me if I thought she would take the ring. I told him I didn't know he would have to ask her himself. He asked her and she said yes. Everyone thought they would someday be married.

Dianna had been in church choir all her life when she realized that she could sing as well as anyone on the radio. She came to me and told me that she wanted to sing on the stage.

I knew a man named Johnny High who had a wonderful stage show at the Will Rodgers Auditorium in Fort Worth. I told her to go audition and just see what he thought about her talent.

Johnny held auditions every Saturday morning, so she drove to Fort Worth by herself and met with Johnny. He had her to sing in his office accompanied by a young guitarist named Joey Floyd.

When Johnny heard Dianna, he told her that she was not only very talented, but that she was also beautiful enough to be in the Miss Texas Pageants. Johnny put her in his show for the next Saturday night, something he never did for a new artist, but he was convinced that she could win Miss Texas and he wanted to get her prepared for the upcoming pageants

It didn't take Johnny long to make all the connections that were needed for Dianna to begin training for the pageants. At the time, Dianna was also in drill team and had an extremely full schedule. Brack loved Dianna with an innocent heart and thought they were to be together all their lives.

When she began going to rehearsals and exercise classes for the pageants, her time for Brack became less and less.

Over time, Brack became extremely jealous of her time with other men. He couldn't stand to see her in rehearsals standing next a man.

While at school one day, Brack confronted Dianna and told her to quit singing. Dianna told him no, and threw the ring at him. The ring was lost.

Brack was expelled from school and began drinking and doing drugs. He told everyone that he did this because of Dianna. His parents hated Dianna for the way Brack was behaving; they decided he needed to go to a drug rehab.

After a few months in rehab, Brack returned home. He tried to follow Dianna around town to get her to quit singing and go back to him.

She wouldn't have anything to do with him because of his attitude about her music and his jealousy.

Dianna made a decision to stop drill team at the last game of the season. That night when the drill team bus pulled into the school parking lot, Brack was waiting for Dianna to get off the bus. She wasn't on the bus. Brack asked two young men and three young girls to join him since he couldn't find Dianna.

They decided to go to Wet Willie's bar to get liquor east of Weatherford on Interstate 20. On the way to the bar, Brack allowed one of the young girls to drive his car.

She was not licensed and had no driving experience. At the time, the state was building loop 820. The girl was driving along the access road next to Interstate 20. It was paved with concrete to about seventy-five feet of the new bridge, and then it turned into gravel.

She was driving at a high rate of speed when she hit the gravel causing the car to flip over and hit the bridge and burst into flames killing all but one of the kids. Brack was seated in the front middle of the car and didn't have a chance to survive the accident.

The next morning was Saturday. We all slept late and as I was making coffee, the phone rang. It was my friend Sherry. She sounded sad and said she had something to tell me.

Weatherford was a small town in the '80s and everyone knew about Brack and Dianna. She said, "Brack, got killed last night." I couldn't move.

Brack and I had been as close as mother and son before all the drama started with the music career. How was I ever going to be able to tell Dianna or my sons? Brack lived with us for a short time.

He and David slept in the same bed. David loved Brack as much as we did.

I waited until Dianna woke up and came into the kitchen before I could manage to say anything. When she came into the kitchen I said, "Dianna, I have something I must tell you."

There was no way to prepare her for this tragic news. I said, "Brack got killed last night." She just looked at me, and then went to her room to get ready for the day. I didn't see her cry at all. Although I knew how much she really loved this young man, there were no tears.

Later that day, we went to the funeral home to visit. When we got there, the funeral director asked us, "Who are you?" I told him that we are the Littlepage's and Dianna was his girlfriend.

The funeral director told us that Brack's mother told him that Dianna Littlepage was not allowed to get near anything concerning Brack. I knew that Dianna had to have some kind of closure.

I told the funeral director and he said, "Okay, I can show you something." He left and came back with an 8x10 picture of Brack, the same picture Brack and Dianna had bought matching shirts for his senior year photograph. Dianna turned and ran from the room.

She left in her mustang and I didn't see her the rest of the day. I waited for her until very late in the evening. She finally came home and walked into the living room. I ask if she was okay and she just looked at me and said yes and went to her room. We didn't go to the funeral.

After that, Dianna moved to Arlington to live with my parents to attend college as we moved to Graham, Texas. Dianna called me often to tell me of young men she met at school.

Every time she would say, "Momma, he looks just like Brack." When she would bring them to Graham to meet us, they didn't look anything like Brack! I knew she was in need of help, but I didn't have any idea what to do for her.

This went on for at least ten years. This was the first time I started thinking about how Satan was trying to invade our family, especially Dianna. All I could do was to pray for Dianna to be okay.

Dianna decided to quit college and go to Nashville. That's where she met Steve, her first husband.

She called me and told me that she had gotten pregnant. They were discussing abortion and she was torn about it. I told her that was the wrong thing to do. The baby was meant to be and that is not what she should do. After looking at a couple of clinics, Dianna decided she wanted to keep her baby.

She called me and asked if they could come home and get married. I told her we would give her a beautiful wedding, just come on home.

CHAPTER VI

Moving On

After I graduated from Weatherford Junior College, Glenn made the announcement that we were moving to Graham, Texas. I refused and told him I wanted to finish school.

I needed to go to UTA in Arlington, Texas. He told me if I wanted to do that, then he would take my children and move to Graham without me. That was absolutely out of the question. I wouldn't leave my children.

I told him if he would allow Dianna to graduate Weatherford High School, then I would move with him. He agreed, and said he would build my dream home when we got there. So I agreed.

I didn't want her to have to leave her friends from Weatherford her last year. We moved after her graduation from high school.

Again, I found myself living in an old, smelly house. This house belonged to his grandfather. It was what is commonly known as a "shotgun house."

We lived in it for about nine months, because unlike every other time, Glenn kept his word about building my dream home. He bought thirty acres and built on top of the hill in front of the Breckenridge Hwy and Murray Road.

Everyone must have thought, "Oh my, those are some rich folks living in that house." Glenn thought by leaving the real estate business in Weatherford, he would surely prosper in the oil business in Graham.

His brothers were making a fine living. What he didn't take into consideration was they had established themselves for years, had secretaries, and put in the hard work to have their businesses. This was something Glenn knew nothing about.

He worked for Bell Helicopter for fifteen years before he quit going into business with Vestie. I paid all the bills and took care of taxes of which he knew nothing.

While in Graham, Glenn made just enough money to keep our unities paid, fuel in our vehicles, and food on our table. We did, however, find the First Methodist Church to attend.

This was the church for us. At least, I thought so at first Everyone was nice and friendly and wore the best of clothes. Glenn and I had plenty to wear, but our sons, on the other hand, were growing out of their clothes. Matthew grew into David's clothes, but David had no one's to grow into.

One Sunday, David couldn't find a pair of pants that would fit him or didn't have holes in them. He was forced to wear what he had. He was so embarrassed, he wouldn't go into his Sunday school room. He stood out in the hallway until it was over. When I realized what he had done, I took money to buy a new pair of pants that fit him properly.

Glenn really didn't want to go to the Methodist church, but he went with the family. One day, he came home from his office for lunch and as we were walking to the front porch for him to leave, he wanted to kiss me goodbye.

When he came toward me I said, "Please don't, I hate to kiss you with that tobacco in your mouth." I told him, "If he would just quit chewing, I would go to whatever church he wanted to go."

He took it out of his mouth and threw it and the new can of tobacco like a Frisbee as far away as he could. And he never dipped again. You could say chewing tobacco is what got me to learn more about God!

We started going to the church all his family attended, Faith Center Assembly of God. It was a great church. This was the first time I really started learning to live on faith.

From week to week, we never knew how much money we would have or how we would buy food for our family. But I never had the worries about that after learning how God took care of the children in the dessert. I trusted God would take care of us. Tithing was something I had done ever since I was a young girl. I knew God said, "Would a man rob God?" And I certainly didn't want to do that. So whatever money Glenn brought in I tithed from it.

I tried to make our life in this beautiful home a wonderful time for our family. Glenn found ways to bring just enough money into our household to support our needs.

Sometimes, someone who must have known our situation would make a love offering to us through the church. One day when church was over, I invited Brenda Romine and her family to come to our home to eat lunch. She said, "What can I bring?" I told her whatever she wanted.

Another person overheard me invite her and asked, "Can we come too?" I said, "Sure." That became the thing to do every Sunday after church since we had such a fine home everyone enjoyed coming.

The kids especially loved the pool table and games. Everyone had a great time in the dream home that Glenn built for us.

I would tell everyone to take the leftovers home and they would say, "No, you keep them." That gave us enough food for a week. That's when I realized that God was truly taking care of us. I didn't have to worry about having enough food anymore.

Somehow enough money came into our household to pay for everything we needed. Our boys had clothes and we were able to buy David a nice pickup to drive. Our family needed nothing! Even Glenn and I were doing much better as a couple.

Glenn had put our home on an interim loan at the bank. For nine years, the bank allowed this loan to exist. Each year, Glenn paid the interest only, so I never had to make a monthly house payment. I didn't know how Glenn accomplished this, and I never ask.

We lived in Graham for nine more years. Then, suddenly we realized the oil business was failing us as the real estate had. Glenn ended up filing for bankruptcy and the bank foreclosed on our home. This seemed to be the worst thing that could happen to us. I never knew how much stress things like that caused.

Our youngest son, Matthew, was about to graduate Graham High School. I prayed that God would allow us to stay in our home until he graduated. Again, God heard and answered my prayer. We got evicted in June after Matt graduated in May.

Matthew wanted to attend Lincoln Tech in Arlington Texas after graduation. I told him I would go with him to find a nice apartment in Arlington. When I found just what he needed, I had the bright idea to fix it up for me to visit him.

What I decided to do was to move in with him to do his laundry, do the cooking, and keep the apartment clean. I thought he would be delighted at that. Except, he had ideas of leaving home, not taking Momma with him.

He was such a good son that he didn't argue about Momma being there. His schedule was so heavy that he wasn't home much anyway. He left for school by seven in the morning and got out at three, came home for his lunch, and went directly to his job at Fed Ex.

He worked until eleven at night. Matthew paid all the bills, the food, and apartment rent. He not only allowed me to stay with him, which relieved the stress I felt during the bankruptcy, but when he graduated, he returned to Graham to help his father any way he could.

CHAPTER VII

Making Peace

During the time we lived in Graham, I didn't think much of Mike until we had our twenty-fifth class reunion. I had the same excited about this reunion as I had for all the previous ones. I knew I would see Mike again.

At the reunion, I saw Mike and we visited. Again, I only told him the good things about my marriage and Glenn's business, nothing that was negative.

Before the reunion was over, Mike came up to me and handed me his business card with his address and cell handwritten on the back. He told me if I ever needed help of any kind to give him a call. I said, thank you and we parted.

Several months later, Glenn found himself being sued by an investor from Boston. We had no money for an attorney and didn't know what we were going to do.

When Glenn turned to me and said, "Barbara, call your friend who's an attorney and ask him what he thinks we should do." I was excited and shocked that Glenn wanted me to call Mike.

I called Mike from Glenn's office and told him what the issue was and ask what we should do. He told me and the matter was resolved. I told Mike I was moving to Arlington to help my son and I gave him our phone number in the apartment. I told him if he needed to reach me that was where I would be.

A couple of months went by, I was living in Arlington and going to Business College while Matt went to Lincoln Tech. One evening while Matt was at his job, I was studying in the living room when the phone rang.

I answered it and a strong manly voice said, "Is Barbara Littlepage there?" I answered, "This is she." He said, "This is Michael Gilmore." I nearly choked on my drink. I couldn't believe my ears. I was delighted to hear his voice.

We talked approximately two hours about everything and nothing. Finally, at about ten thirty, I told him that my son would soon the coming home and I didn't want to be on the phone when he came in.

Mike said, "May I tell you something before we hang up?" I said, "Yes, certainly." Mike told me that he had loved me from the moment he first laid eyes on me, he loved me now, and he would love me till the day he died.

I was totally in shock. I couldn't say anything except "Thank you and good bye." I never told Mike how I felt about him and never saw him again for many years. I think I saw him at all the other reunions, but we didn't say much to each other except hello.

Finally, on our fiftieth class reunion 2014, Mike and I texted each other and we agreed that we would see meet at the party the evening before the reunion. We each planned to bring our spouses to the party.

Both Mike's wife and Glenn had a call to work that took them away for the evening. When Glenn got the call to leave, I decided not to go to the party. I texted Mike and told him I wasn't coming and he agreed also not to go.

I worked until about five thirty in the afternoon. A friend from church came to visit. I was really tired and didn't feel like going to the party. As we sat and talked, my energy began coming back. She asks me if I thought I could go to the party, and I told her I did feel better. I called my girlfriend and ask if she was going to the party and she told me yes she was, but she would be late.

I decided to go and told her I would be there, but also late. By that time, it was 7:15, the party started at 7:30. I didn't text Mike, so I didn't expect to see him that night. I arrived 8:15 p.m.

When I walked in, I thought, "Oh my, I'm in the wrong room, all these people are old." When I entered the room, I spotted my girlfriend near the back of the room. I started working my way to where she was when I noticed a man standing with his back to me.

I had no idea who he was. As I got behind him, he turned around and it was Mike. At the last minute, we both changed our minds about going and didn't tell each other. We were so happy to see each other that we embraced tightly.

I told Mike I needed to say hi to my girlfriend, and I would be right back. When I came back, he asked if he could buy me a tea and I said, "Yes, please." When he left, I felt like a teenager again. I was so excited to be able to talk with him without our spouses.

After all these years, I decided I wanted to tell Mike about the turn of events back in 1964. I wanted him to know that I always loved him, but just couldn't tell him during that time.

I wanted him to know that he was the one I wanted to marry and have a family. He was so forgiving and told me I should have told him. He said we would have worked it out. And he wouldn't be ashamed of me for what happened.

I told him I thought he was so young and that I would ruin his life if I told him and he tried to help me. I didn't want to be the reason his career choice may have been affected.

I told Mike about our church and that I couldn't accept being the pastor because I felt ashamed about my past. He told me that if anyone was good enough, it would be me. Mike said, "I have known you since you were sixteen and I know what kind of girl you were and still are." He said, "If God would use Saul, He would certainly use Barbara."

After that, I had the peace that I was the one God had chosen to lead the church. For the past two years, I wouldn't acknowledge I could possibly be chosen by God to do such an enormous task for God.

Mike and I still have fond feelings for each other, but we have each taken a vow before God and do not intend on breaking them.

CHAPTER VIII

Step by Step

During the years Glenn was in real estate, he found properties that were something he wanted Tommy, his brother, to invest in with him. Tommy was excited to invest with Glenn.

They purchased two properties together. Tommy provided the financing and Glenn provided all the remodeling and labor. It seemed like a fair trade for the investments that were made.

At the time, Tommy took care of the legal side of the investments. Tommy was an oil man who had an attorney on staff. When the attorney handled the paperwork, he put the investments in Tommy's name only. Glenn never thought to ask about whose name the properties were in until several years later.

Glenn found out that everything was in Tommy's name and told me about it. I said to him, "You need to get your name put on the property deeds that you and Tommy bought together," because if something happened to Tommy, his family wouldn't know that you should have a part of it.

Glenn answered me back by saying, "I'm not going to worry about that because God is in control." He knew his brother wouldn't hurt us intentionally.

When Glenn was going through the bankruptcy, Tommy came to Glenn and told him he realized what Glenn and I were going through. Tommy had sold Glenn the property to build our dream home on and he offered to buy back the surrounding twenty-nine acres that were not being foreclosed on. Without Tommy, we would have been totally broke.

Then Tommy also gave Glenn his choice of one of the two investment properties they bought all those years ago, paid in full and taxes paid I wanted the town property because the country property had nothing on it.

The town property was the Westgate Professional Building and the country property was the Brock property. I thought it was too far out in the country, but Glenn wanted it, so I decided to honor Glenn's choice and, again, I agreed to move onto the property that Glenn wanted.

We had a lot of clearing to do to make the land buildable so we started clearing with the only tools we had—hand saws. One day, a man drove onto our property and got out of his pickup carrying a beer in one hand and a cigarette in the other.

I am highly allergic to cigarettes and I don't drink beer, so I turned away when he walked up. Thank God Glenn greeted him neighborly and they talked for awhile.

J.W. Matthews was the man's name. He told Glenn that he had driven by our property several times and noticed us trying to clear the property. He said that there was no way we could get it cleared the way we were doing it.

He said he had a bulldozer and if we would allow him to bring it here, he would just play on our property and clean it up. Thank God Glenn did what he did because Mr. Matthews cleared every bit of our property at no charge! He wouldn't even accept fuel money.

I could see God's hand on everything we did. I believe it all started because I put God first, I tithed, kept my vow, I honored our parents, and I also honored Glenn when the choice came where to live. I believe putting God first, tithing, keeping vows, and honoring our parents was the real key to any success I've had.

We still didn't know what kind of job we would be able to do. When we moved onto the Brock property, both Matthew and Glenn tried to find jobs to no avail.

At the time, we lived in a small twenty-year-old, thirty-foot travel trailer house that our son David bought for his job on the pipeline. He had just bought a new trailer when we needed a place to live. Again, I found myself in a not-so-fine home, but with all that had happened, I was glad to have a roof over my head.

The trailer wasn't the best, but we made the best of it. The refrigerator was broken, but I had my own. We found a pallet and placed it outside at the end of the trailer and put my refrigerator on it. Every time I needed anything, I had to go outside to get it, even in the rain or snow!

There was a well on the property. It was the only source of water, but there was no stand or tank. Tommy gave Glenn a water stand and a five-hundred-gallon tank for it.

When Glenn and Matthew got it installed, they found that the pump wouldn't work. Glenn contacted a man named Herbert Walker who worked on wells for him in the past.

Mr. Walker put a new pump on the well and gave us the bad news that there was just no water in the well. Glenn paid him and told him thank you for trying to get it working.

Glenn had a friend named Richard who owned the KOA camp in Weatherford. He asked him if we paid fifty dollars a month, would Richard let our family have unlimited showers and water to drink. Richard said, "Sure."

We did this for months, until one day I was so tired of hauling water in, and having to carry my shampoo and towels to the KOA for showers. I told Glenn that I had married him for better or worse and this was the worse, I wanted water on this place! I didn't know things could get a whole lot worse, but they can!

Glenn's reply back to me was if you want water on this place, then just go out there and pray for it! I grabbed his hand and shouted, "If any two or three pray for anything in Jesus' name, it shall be done!"

I pulled him out to the well and began praying. I shouted to the Lord, "I need water. I am thirsty and dirty and I need water, in the name of Jesus, Amen!"

I turned to Glenn and told him, "Let's go to Wal-Mart." At the time, Wal-Mart was where the Tractor Supply is now. We shopped for about two hours when we returned our humble home it was dark.

When we drove into the driveway, I could hear water splashing against the cement below the well. I told Glenn to turn his headlights on the well. He did and water was running over the top of the tank!

There was no water in the well, but when I prayed, God heard me and answered with the water. We had water for as long as we needed it.

One day, Glenn sold something that made us $1,500.00, which was the amount the co-op told me it would cost for running the water tap from the top of the hill to our property.

The well water tasted good, but was sandy. As quickly as I got the money, I went to the co-op office and paid to have the water line brought to our property.

As soon as the line was installed, our water tank went dry. God provided for us as long as we needed the water from the well, when we didn't need it any longer the well dried up.

Later, I was at the KOA office visiting with Richard when I heard a voice calling my name. I looked around to see Mr. Walker, the water well man. He was saying hi to me.

When I told him the story of the water, he said to me, "If you have that much power with the Lord, please keep my kids in your prayers." I told him I would pray for his children, but he had the authority to claim his children for the Lord and to pray for them anytime he wanted.

I attended a Kenneth Copeland rally where John Avanzeny was preaching at the Fort Worth Convention Center. John asks everyone who didn't have a house to raise their hands. I wasn't embarrassed because there were at least ten thousand people there and I didn't know any of them. So I raised my hand.

Then, John asks who wants a house paid in full in one year? Again, I raised my hand. John said, "You could ask anything in Jesus' name and it shall be done." So, as I sat there all alone among the ten thousand, I ask in Jesus' name for a house paid in full in one year and I expected it.

As time went on, our friend, Don Eichler, came to visit us one day and told us of a house in a Mineral Wells pasture. He took Glenn to look at it. Glenn came home and told me about it so my sister Joyce and I went to look at it.

When my sister and I got to the location of the house, it was in the middle of a pasture setting high on blocks. It was too high for either Joyce or me to climb up on, so Joyce boosted me up on the porch and I pulled her up behind me.

Glenn thought I wouldn't like the house because it was a small two-bedroom home built on the style of a Jim Walter's home. The house was finished on the outside, but not on the inside. It did have wiring and framed walls. When I saw it, I could envision it exactly like it turned out, a beautifully decorated home.

Mr. Crawford, the man who built the house, tried to start a business by building these houses He built five homes. Four sold and one sat in the pasture for five years. Again, I saw evidence of God taking care of us.

Glenn asked me how much he should offer on the house. I told him that we only had six thousand dollars and we couldn't offer much because we had to pay someone to move it to our property.

The next day, he went to the office of the builder and he offered three thousand for the house. Mr. Crawford told him that he had twelve thousand in the material, there was no way he could take that. Glenn thanked him and returned to our property.

That evening, Glenn and I prayed over how much more to offer, then went to sleep. The next morning, Glenn again went to offer what we decided on. He offered four thousand dollars.

Mr. Crawford said, "Glenn, I already told you I had twelve thousand in the house, I can't take that." Again, Glenn thanked him and started to walk out of his office when he called out, "Glenn, come back, I will take four thousand for the house."

Another miracle! We were able to pay cash for a nice house. Although, then we had to find someone who would move it for the remaining two thousand dollars.

Glenn remembered a man named David Bailey who had moved mobile homes, so he called him to ask how much he would move our house from Mineral Wells to our Brock property. The mover told Glenn seven hundred dollars and he would set it up for Glenn. What a blessing!

This home was probably my favorite of all the homes we had. This time, it was paid in full when we moved into it within a year. It was only two bedrooms, but we loved it. Matthew had his room and Glenn and I had ours. God surely kept us in His hands!

By this time, we had started going to Peaster Baptist Church. This church was something like Faith Center in Graham, Tex. We were there every time the doors were open. We made lots of friends and thought we would never leave this church.

Our daughter Dianna had begun an exciting singing career. She was fairly well known in the Nashville, Fort Worth Stockyard and Dallas music scene. By this time, she had married and divorced twice. She desperately wanted to serve God, but couldn't manage to pay bills singing in church.

Finally, she made the decision to quit the bars and go to church and take whatever other jobs she could to pay bills. She met a nice young man named Randy and they got married.

Randy worked at a warehouse driving a forklift. Dianna relied on Randy to help her with the bills, only problem was Randy made minimum wage. There just wasn't enough money. The first week he came in with his paycheck and handed it to her, she regretted her decision to marry. She was impulsive every time she decided to marry.

Randy had never gone to a church like Peaster. He was a nervous wreck when people started trying to become friends with him. As time went on, Randy made friends and felt at home and was well-liked by the people there.

When Dianna made the announcement that she and Randy were getting a divorce, the church turned against Dianna. She had been asked to be the special singer in the Christmas program, but when the pastor heard what she had done concerning Randy, he uninvited her to sing that year.

Our whole family attended that church. The devil was really beginning to show me that he was attacking our family with full force. We were in that church for about nine years when each of the family quit going. I'm sure Satan thought he was winning.

While we were going to Peaster, I had an experience that again showed me that I was highly favored by God. One Sunday as Glenn and I were walking though the parking lot, I saw a white Lincoln with a "for sale" sign on it.

I had always wanted a white Lincoln. As I walked past the car, I laid my hands on it and I said, "In the name of Jesus, I claim this car." I took the number on the sign and called after church. The lady told me they wanted $12,000.00 for the car. I sure didn't have that kind of money, but that didn't stop me from desiring it.

The next day, I went to see the banker. He told me if I could come up with $2,000, he would loan me the rest. Our business was just beginning to make good money, but within the time period I needed to raise the down payment, we didn't do very much business. I was becoming discouraged about getting the down payment when David came to visit me.

He asked me if I was able to come up with the down payment yet. I told him, "No, I sure couldn't." He said, "I am so sorry. I know how you wanted that car." Then he left.

After a while, I saw the shadow of a man walking toward my kitchen door. It was David. He came back to tell me that he just sold something and he had the $2,000 I needed. Praise God, I got my car. This was just the first of many things I desired and got. I knew if I "delighted myself in the Lord I could have the desires of my heart." By this time, I couldn't deny that God was watching out for me.

CHAPTER IX

Walking in Faith

My parents had another child when I was five years old. Her name was Patty. Patty was born with learning and physical disabilities. When Patty turned twenty-one, my parents decided to put her in a home for "people like her." Momma tried to work and she had problems finding someone to watch Patty. Patty had a well-formed body, and on more than one occasions, the son of the lady who was supposed to be watching Patty molested her.

Momma and Daddy thought Patty would be safer in a state home. When they called me to tell me about putting Patty into a home, I begged them not to do that, because I thought Patty would be hurt. I wanted Patty to move into my house, but Momma thought that she was keeping that burden off of me. I never thought of Patty as a burden!

As time went on, Patty was moved from Fort Worth State School to Denton State School and in each case, Patty told me about men "touching" her. Momma and Daddy moved Patty every time they learned of this.

About fifteen years after Patty was put into the home, she was infected with AIDS. We lived in Graham when I learned of this. This was another time Momma couldn't tell me the news. She stayed in the kitchen while Daddy took me to the couch in front of our fireplace and said to me, "Bobbie, there is something I need to tell you. Patty has AIDS." He also said, "We will keep her away from your family." I told him, "No, you will not!" She is my sister and we will continue to have visits with her.

My heart was so angry at my parents for putting her in a home and not allowing her to live with me. I wanted to scream out, "I told you so." But I didn't. It was then that Daddy said something to me I never expected to hear. He said, "Bobbie, I so am sorry for putting you in the cellar when you were little."

One evening, he and momma were arguing, daddy never hit our mother, but he would take his anger out on Joyce and me. I don't know what I did to make him angry at me, but he grabbed my right arm and dragged me through the house and out the door. He opened the cellar door and put me down in there, and he said he was putting a big rock on the door so I couldn't get out. I saw spider webs and I thought there were snakes in the cellar. I was petrified.

I screamed and screamed and banged on the door. I don't think he left me in the cellar for long, but it still caused me a lot of trauma.

That happened when I was about four years old. For about forty years, I had nightmares because of what he did all those years ago. I never told him how badly he scared me. When I had the nightmares, I would wake up screaming and begging Glenn to "please put a light in my casket. I don't want to be in the dark."

For all those years, I tried to forgive daddy in my heart, but I just couldn't because he never mentioned it after it happened until now. Instantly, I forgave him. And just as instantly, the nightmare stopped. That taught me the power of forgiveness.

It was then that I knew I had to forgive my parents for putting Patty in a home. Step by step, I began to realize that God knows everything that we must endure and he is going to allow it for our good and for His glory.

CHAPTER X

Keeping the Faith

After our family left Peaster, we stayed out of church for a while. Then we found a small church that was held at the Twentieth Century building. The pastor and his family were friendly and we enjoyed being a part of it.

While attending the small church in Weatherford, I asked the pastor's wife "Is someone with AIDS welcomed into this church?" Her answer was, "It depends on how they got it." I couldn't see how it was relevant. That shouldn't have mattered! This was another response from a church leader that made me ill. I didn't think Jesus would have asked anyone how they became ill before He healed them.

One day as I was cleaning my kitchen, I was looking out the window over the sink and I had a thought or message from God. I heard that I needed to build onto my house, because there were three people that I would need to care for.

They were my Daddy, Momma, and Dianna. This was about 1998. I told Glenn that God had given me the message that I would have to care for these three family members and we needed to build onto our house. He knew how God had been speaking to me and he said, "Well, let's get started building."

We added an additional bedroom, large bathroom for handicapped people, and a large living room. I made the doors to the bedroom double-wide in order to be able to get in and out with a hospital bed. No one needed that at the time, but I had heard God and I wanted to be prepared.

About 2005, daddy became very ill with COPD and heart trouble. He was in the hospital for about three months straight. By the third month, both Momma and I were worn out from staying with him at the hospital every day.

Finally, Daddy was moved to a rehab center in Fort Worth when he seemed to be doing better. I thought Momma needed a bed to rest on when she was with him so I bought a folding bed for her to use. One day, before I could get to the hospital, she called me and asked if I would take her to lunch. That was what I intended to do when I got there.

When I arrived, she was sleeping on the bed and Daddy was also asleep. I didn't want to disturb her so I sat quietly in a chair next to her. After a while, she woke up and said, "Oh you're here, let me go to the restroom and freshen up and we can go."

I took her to the Luby's Cafeteria near the hospital. We got our food and each carried our own tray to a table near the front next to a window.

As we were eating our lunch, I was telling her about property I had bought to build a steak house. I thought that our daughter Dianna could have a nice place to sing and we could have another business that would profit our whole family.

Momma responded to what I was saying with a nod or an answer when suddenly she stopped eating and responding.

I grabbed her face and screamed "Momma!" and she just sat there. Her eyes were open, but she couldn't speak. People from all around the cafeteria ran over to help, but they could do nothing. The ambulance was called and she was taken to Medical Plaza Hospital. Momma had a major stroke.

Now as Daddy was getting better, Momma had a stroke and I had two parents in two different hospitals. The doctor at Medical Plaza told me that I needed to let Momma "pass away gently." I asked him how long it took to "pass away gently" and he told me about eighteen or nineteen days.

I asked him if she would get any food or water and he told me "No." I told him that wasn't passing gently, that was starving her to death.

I demanded that he put a feeding tube into her stomach and I would take her home. He told me there was no way I could care for my mother and I told him to do what I said and I would take her home the next day.

I didn't know how I would care for her, but I knew God had told me to do that. That day, I made arrangements for Holland Lake Nursing to get a two-bedroom ready because I was moving both my parents there the next day.

Momma was in a coma for about two months. She and Daddy were in the same room. Daddy seemed to come back to health while Momma was unconscious. I stayed in the room with them during the day for about a month.

One day, I came to the room and told Daddy that I could no longer come to the nursing home and I was taking them home. Daddy looked sad and said, "Baby, I can't take care of me and Momma. I can't go home," I just laughed and told him I was taking both of them to my house. He looked like a little boy who just gotten a new toy. He had a smile across his face that was beautiful.

That day, I got Daddy and his things and I took him to my house. I had the front bedroom neat as a pin. I wanted Daddy to feel like he was in the Hilton. I left Momma at the nursing home for an additional day until I could get a hospital bed delivered to our house.

The next day, I went to the nursing home to check on my mother about 10:00 a.m. When I walked into her room, I noticed she was moving her right hand back and forth though her hair.

She must have regained consciousness and realized that there was something in her diaper, because she had put her hand into it and came out with feces all over her hand. She rubbed it all over her face and hair. I came out of her room screaming, "Somebody better get my momma cleaned up now!"

I was so upset that nobody had been watching her I demanded to have her released that morning. I had just gotten her bed into my home, but didn't have the wheelchair that was needed by a paralyzed person.

I told the nurse I was taking the wheelchair she had been using at the home and the nurse told me, no, I couldn't take it. I just said, "Stand there and watch me." I took my momma to the car and also took the wheel chair.

Daddy recovered from not being able to walk and drooling on himself, to being a happy, well-adjusted, healthy man within just a week or two. When I got him home, he was taking about eighteen different drugs. One evening while the home health nurse was there, she, daddy, Glenn, and I sat at the kitchen table and read the side effects of the drugs he was taking.

I would ask Daddy, "Do you want these side effects?" He would answer no and he would shove them away. Daddy was down to about three drugs the nurse, he, and I thought he needed. After that, he was feeling great.

One day, I took daddy to get a manicure and a pedicure with me. He had never had one before. You would have thought he was a king sitting there with me in that pedi-chair getting his feet massaged. I only wish I had taken pictures. He was so cute.

I got daddy a motorized wheelchair so that he wouldn't have to walk if he felt he couldn't. I think he felt he couldn't when maybe he could have. He really enjoyed his wheelchair.

He would get into it and drive out the front door of our living room to the parking lot and do wheelies. I would stand on the sidewalk and beg him to be careful and not have a wreck. He just laughed at me and kept it up. He liked the attention he was getting.

Finally, one day, daddy said to me, "Bobbie, get ready. I want to go to Grand Prairie." I said, okay and I called a friend to sit with Momma while we were gone.

Daddy wanted to go to every bank that he and Momma had any money in and give it to me. The first time he did that I said, "Daddy, don't give your money to me. It's your mad money, you might need it." He just said, "No, baby, as long as I have you, I don't need anything."

Another time, our daughter came to our house and was extremely angry. She came in screaming that I had stolen her money. I didn't know what she was talking about. Then Daddy spoke up and said, "I gave all my money to your momma. I don't have anything else for you."

Daddy had signed over to Glenn and me all the money in his Edward Jones account. We could only imagine that momma might have promised her money from that account before she had the stroke and never told us about it.

At that time, everyone thought daddy would be dead in a short time. Daddy thought that Dianna must have tried to withdraw money and there was none.

Daddy was so upset that he didn't speak for the rest of the day. I was worried about him. The next morning, as I was dusting and cleaning the living room while he was sitting at the kitchen table, he called me to join him.

He said, "I want to give you something else." I said, "Daddy, you don't have anything else to give me."

He had given me all his money, his house, and his car. I thought everything he owned he had already given to me. I said, "What else do you have?" He said, "I have the house that Momma and I bought for Dianna. I want to give it to you."

I said, "Oh no, Daddy you will be starting WWIII." He said, "I didn't start it, she did!" Then, he had me call Jewel, the lady he knew at the title office, to bring the deed transfer papers and he signed the house over to me.

Daddy never tolerated rudeness or disrespect from his children or his grandchildren. He was from a generation where children said yes mam and no mam and he used to say to us, "When I say jump, you better say how high.

I loved Daddy, but he could be very strict when he wanted to. His mind was made up. If I hadn't already used the money that he gave me, I would have gladly given her whatever she needed.

She was in college trying to earn her degree to become an attorney. She also sang and waited tables. I was very proud of her for that. I felt awful that I had spent the money on all my bills.

I did that because I could no longer work during the time I had Momma and Daddy. By paying things off, I didn't have monthly payments during that time.

I thought everything was fine until she came to our house in such a fit. I thought the devil himself had a grasp on her. I could tell her blood pressure was really high by the look on her face. She stormed out to her car and drove off very fast. The only thing I could do was to pray for her.

Daddy died January 2006. He was very healthy and happy to the end. He had congestive heart failure and COPD. At times, he had a hard time breathing, I would administer his breathing treatment and he would be better, but otherwise he was good.

There were no signs of him dying until the day before he died. Daddy lived with me for nine months. Daddy and I got closer than I ever dreamed we would be.

He apologized to me for the way he disciplined us when we were little. He brought up the cellar again and told me how sorry he was that he had done that to me. We had such a healing between us. I only wish all fathers and daughters could end like we did. The only thing that would have been better was if we could have lived that all our lives.

CHAPTER XI

Grieving Loses

Momma came out of the coma about a month after living with us. She realized that she could no longer talk or move as she had before the stroke. She would wail out like a calf crying for its momma. She made long, loud mourning cries as if grieving. The noise was, at times, unbearable. This would go on into the night.

One evening, I asked Daddy if he would like me to move her to the back bedroom so he could get some rest. He said, "No, she is my wife and I won't leave her alone." He wanted her to be by his side always. I never asked him that again.

After about two months of Momma crying, I got her to listen to me. I asked her if she could hear me and she shook her head, "Yes." I told her it did no good for her to cry all the time.

I hated that she had a stroke, but we just needed to move on. I asked again, "Do you understand?" She said yes again. After that, she stopped the crying until her brother or one of her sisters would come to visit.

I would have to kneel beside her and comfort her and let her know that she would make them sad if she didn't stop crying. She would listen, and then she would smile at me and them.

I taught Momma to sign "I love you." We signed that to each other every time I came near her. That was something neither Daddy nor Momma ever told me or my sisters when we were all together.

I wish they would have been able to say the words to us. One evening, as I lay on the couch watching TV, I felt momma staring at me. I looked at her and said, "What are you thinking momma?" She just smiled and signed, "I love you." It was all I could do to not smother her in kisses. I loved my momma so much, but never heard those words from her mouth.

Momma lived another nineteen months, months I wouldn't have had her if I had listened to the doctor. He said I couldn't take care of my momma. Well I proved him wrong! Momma loved football and she, Glenn, and I watched every football game there was. She also loved old movies. I found every old movie I could and we watched them into the night.

After Daddy died, I took Momma and got her a manicure and a pedicure. I don't think she had ever had one before. She smiled all the time we were there. I did whatever I could to make her life as good as possible while she was with me.

Momma had wanted to bury Daddy next to my sister Patty in the Arlington cemetery. She bought enough lots for her children and their husbands.

While Daddy was gravely ill, before he came to stay with me, his mother, my Grandma Phillips, and his sisters, all begged me to ask Momma to bury Daddy in the Weatherford cemetery.

I told them that I would ask Momma, but I knew what her answer would be. I never had the opportunity to ask her that question because she had the stroke before I could.

The day she had the stroke I went back to the rehab hospital to tell Daddy that she had a stroke and the doctor told me she would die very soon. He asked me then to bury her at Weatherford and bring Patty to Weatherford also.

He always wanted to be buried by his brother and his dad, but Momma never gave that a thought.

As soon as I got Momma and Daddy to my house, I started making arrangement to move Patty's body to Weatherford so Daddy could see that I had done as he requested. I had no idea it would take so long to move a body, but it did.

It was exactly nine months to get the body moved. The day before Daddy, died I got her moved to Weatherford. I came into the house and kneeled at his side and I said, "Daddy, I got her moved. She is beside where you and Momma will be." He was so weak, but a big smile came over his face.

That night, Daddy asked me to sleep with him. I said, "Daddy, I can't sleep with you because your breathing machine is so loud." I was always so tired I needed to sleep when I could. The next night, I decided I didn't care about getting sleep, I just needed to do what Daddy ask of me. I slept with Daddy the night before he died. He always wore muscle shirts. He had a rash on his chest. As I lay next to him, I scratched his chest to soothe him.

I said, "Daddy, I sure love you." He said back to me, "I sure love you, too, baby girl." Oh my God, if only those words had come out while we were all young how much better our lives would have been. I'm just grateful that I honored my Daddy as I did, or I may never have hard those words.

I always needed to hear that from him. He was my hero. I remember one day, I was standing in the front yard of our house in Grand Prairie, I was about eleven years old. Daddy ran up behind me and picked me up over his head. I thought he was "Superman." I loved him so much, but we never told each other. I think he thought that was a word only for his wife.

Daddy did something else for his girls to show his love. He built a playhouse for us. I remember he let us help him. We had a great time in that little house. One time, Daddy had a flock of turkey. The turkey always chased Patty. One of the turkeys chased her into the playhouse. She dove into one of the windows and the turkey pecked her on the butt. We all came running, but stopped to laugh. It was so funny. We did run the turkey away. Poor Patty scared her half to death.

Another thing Daddy did for us was build a little car. Patty had a toy Jeep that was red and yellow. Daddy decided he could build one for us. It was just like the toy, except it had a Cushman scooter motor in it and it would run.

One day, Patty, Joyce and I decided to drive it to town. We got it started and off we went. We were doing just fine until Joyce looked back and saw Momma driving after us.

She made us turn around and go back to our neighborhood. She didn't get mad at us. She was just glad we were all okay. Momma and Daddy showed their love in so many ways. We just never heard the word "love."

Another day, I came home from school and Momma had a beautiful pale blue dress with sequins all over it. She bought it for me to have for a school dance.

I didn't think I would be able to go to the dance because we couldn't afford a dress for me, but somehow she found the money and I had the most beautiful dress at the dance. I felt like a princess.

Other times I thought momma was being mean to me. She wouldn't let Daddy buy a little Nash Cosmopolitan car for me. I was so angry until I heard her tell daddy that she didn't want me to be killed in a small car like that. I'm sure that was her way of saying "I love Barbara and want her to live." I never got a car, but I lived through that. Some of my friends didn't live through high school.

CHAPTER XII

More Tragedy

Daddy had been gone for a little over a month when it was Valentine's Day. I went by to visit Grandma Phillips, who was nearly 102 years old. She lived in Fort Worth. I asked her if she would please come to visit me and spend the night at my house.

She had never stayed overnight with me, although I used to stay with her when I was a child. I had the feeling I needed to be with her. She told me that she would love to come and spend the night with me.

She came with my aunt Evelyn. Evelyn asked grandma if she would like to stop at the Dollar Store to get flowers to put on Daddy's grave. Grandma told her, "No, I just want to get to Barbara's house."

Grandma was upset because my Aunt Lorene had tried to take her purse away. Grandma said, "I hope I never see her again." I tried to comfort her and told her that my aunt was wrong by trying to take away her purse.

She seemed to calm down and we had a wonderful evening after that. We talked about when Daddy was young and she looked at all the pictures I had around the living room. She said, "He was so handsome," and of course Evelyn and I agreed.

That night, Grandma got ready for bed and I decided I wanted to get into bed with her like I did as a child. I peeked into her room and asked, "Grandma, are you awake?" She answered, "Yes, I am." I said, "May I get into bed with you?" And she said, "Yes," and pulled the covers back for me to get in.

We talked for a long time just like we used to when I was a child. Grandma was good at talking. She used to talk me to sleep. That night, I told her I wanted her to come back again to visit and I was going to call this room "Grandma's room."

She was delighted with that. She said, "You really want me to come spend more nights at your house?" I said, "Absolutely, I do." With that I told her good night and I went to my own bed.

The next morning, I got up early and left for work. I didn't want to disturb her. I came back to my house about noon. She and my aunt were just eating their breakfast.

I was preparing lunch for Glenn and me. My aunt decided that she wanted to take a shower. So grandma went to the living room to watch TV while I prepared lunch.

The home health nurse came in about that time. She was tending to Momma's needs. After a while, I heard grandma let out a loud belch. I said, "Grandma, what did you eat to make you do that?" She said, "I don't know." Then she did it again.

I came into the living room to check on her and she said she was feeling a pain in her chest and needed to use the restroom. I offered to get the potty chair and bring it to the living room, but she said,

"No, I won't use it in the living room." Again, I offered to help her into the bedroom, but she said, "No, I will walk on my own."

Evelyn had just gotten out of the shower when grandma belched loudly again. Evelyn asked grandma if she was okay and grandma said, "I'm okay" We asked if she wanted to go to the hospital and she said, "No, I'll be okay."

Evelyn went into her room to get dressed, again grandma belched real loud. She took a very deep breath and held it. I yelled, "I think grandma is dying." Evelyn said, "Did you say grandma died?" I said, "No, but I think she's dying." Evelyn screamed, "Call 911." So, I did. I will never do that again, if someone is as old as grandma was.

The paramedics came and forced me to let them tend to grandma. They cut her clothes off and began beating on her chest. I screamed, "Don't do that to her. If she's not dead, she will be after you finish with her."

I jumped on the bed and began holding on to her. They told me to get off her because they were getting ready to shock her and if I didn't get off they would shock me too. I got off and just sat there watching as they did what they said they had to do, because I called them. I will never do that again.

Grandma died February 16, 2006 as I watched them abuse her. Again, I was in bed with my loved one as they passed to the other side.

This was the second time I was holding my loved one as they passed. But it wasn't the last time. Momma lived another twelve months. She passed in February 2007 as I stood at her bedside holding her in my arms.

This time I didn't call 911. I just called the police department and told them my Momma had just died and I needed an ambulance to come get her. I waited and waited, it seemed like a lifetime. It was almost three hours before they came to get her. I cried and cried because now I had none of my parents or grandparents left.

I cried out and asked the Lord why He had me to be the one who ushered each one across and I heard Him say He chose me to do that, This time I not only heard Him tell me that, but also other people told me that as well. This was something I thought I could never do, but I did.

I mourned the loss of my parents and grandma until I couldn't cry any more. I ask Glenn if he and Harold Whitling would build one gazebo for me to go to when I needed to cry, so that I could be away from people.

Harold and Glenn together made an excellent building team. They went onto the internet and found that the Amish people build a grand pavilion. They ask me if I would allow them to build a pavilion, that was three gazebos.

I was in shock, but I answered, yes and off they went building. When the first one was nearly finished, I began holding my hands in the air and praising God. I called it a Praise Pavilion, not a grand pavilion. And that's how the name Praise Pavilion came into existence.

As time went on, I decided to become an ordained minister, just to do weddings. I never wanted a church on our property. I had known of too many preachers who did things that weren't very godly. Since I was not a college trained pastor, I never thought of having a church on the property.

As time went on, people kept on asking me if we were going to have a church at the Praise Pavilion, I would say, "No, I don't like preachers."

Although, I needed a building as a reception hall to hold weddings, I just couldn't make enough money to build the building. Our trucking business had sold five million dollars in freight the year we built the gazebos.

I thought we would always be able to make enough money to build whatever we wanted. But this was 2008 and our business nearly went out of business!

I decided to just wait on the Lord. While I was waiting, I had a dream one night. In this dream, my daughter Dianna had a stroke. I woke up screaming that my daughter had a stroke! Glenn said, "Oh honey that was just a bad dream. Dianna didn't have a stroke."

He said, "Let's pray for her and she will be okay" We prayed. I felt better so I went back to bed. That was in the early hours of Saturday morning. I continued to pray for her until Monday morning while I was at work.

The phone rang and I answered it. A customer wanted me to take a package to Oklahoma City in my little Toyota. I was delighted to get a small package to deliver, which got me out of the office for a day.

As I was coming back home, I had just crossed into Texas when I had a horrible pain shoot through my right temple and the rest of my body so intensely that I had to pull my truck over and stop.

I grabbed the steering wheel and began praying. I said, "Lord, I know this is not my pain, but my child. Please don't let it kill her." As soon as I prayed that prayer, the pain stopped. That happened at 4:00 p.m. I arrived at my office at 6:00 p.m.

I laid my phone and purse on the reception desk in my building. I went into my office and began doing my paperwork for this job. Just then, my cell phone rang.

Glenn was passing as it rang and I asked him to hand it to me. When he answered, I could tell it was Caitlin, our granddaughter, because he always spoke to her in a childish voice. I screamed, "What does she want?" He told me to be quiet so he could hear her.

I grabbed the phone from him. I asked Caitlin what she wanted. Caitlin asks me, "What would make Momma's hands and feet numb and her voice slur?"

I immediately asked to speak to Dianna. I said, "Dianna, tell Momma what is going on." She said in a slurred voice, "My hands and feet are numb and I can't talk." I asked who was with her and she told me, "Jeff." I told her to give Jeff the phone and tell him he needed to get her to the hospital.

We met Jeff and Dianna in the hospital emergency room. Dianna was sitting a wheel chair and Jeff was filling out paperwork. I kneeled down beside her and ask, "Dianna, what time did this happen to you?" She answered at 4 o'clock. I have no doubt that God told me what was to happen so that I could be in prayer for her.

I told the receptionist that she couldn't be left in the lobby. She had a stroke and must be taken in immediately. The nurse was called and Dianna was taken straight to the X-ray room. I stood outside the room and heard the nurses' voices calling for the doctor to get there quickly.

He came rushing into the room and then came rushing out past me. I grabbed him and said, "What are we going to do for her?" He said, "Rush her to Medical Plaza as soon as possible."

She was sent by ambulance. I followed and got to her as soon as she was delivered to the emergency drive. I wanted to hear her voice. I knew Momma couldn't talk at all when she had the stroke. Dianna could still talk.

She was taken into the emergency room for testing. I stayed with her the whole time. By the time we got to the hospital, all her fans and friends who knew her because of her music were there to see her. There were probably a hundred or more people there to hear that she would be okay.

At midnight, the nurse came into the lobby and told everyone except her two closest relatives they needed to leave. The two relatives could come in to tell her goodnight and then they needed to leave also.

Courtney and Caitlin, Dianna's daughters, got up to see their momma. I got in behind them to go into her room also. Caitlin turned around and said to me, "Grandma, the nurse said two." I said, "You're one, Courtney is two and I am Momma, and I'm going in."

The nurse told us we had to leave at midnight. It was five minutes to midnight when we got into her room. The girls were standing to her right and talking to her. Telling her that she was beautiful and the doctor would fix her up and she would be home soon.

I watched the clock until one minute before midnight. Then I said, "Girls, we have to leave in a minute. Tell Mommy goodnight." At that time, Dianna turned her head to the left to see me. I didn't know that she was blind on the left side. She didn't know I was there until I spoke.

When she turned her head to the left, she went into a seizure and began jerking every which way. Her face looked as if a demon had entered her body. I yelled at the girls to go get Daddy and tell the nurse she is having a seizure.

I immediately started praying and screaming at the demons to leave her along, I said, "She is *not* yours, she belongs to the Lord." I kept my arm raised above my head and around her to prevent any demons getting to her.

The nurses came in and gave her a shot of anti-seizure meds. The nurse turned to me and said, "We got to her in three minutes. If it had gone on four minutes, she would have been severely brain damaged. If it had gone on for five minutes, she would have been dead!"

Again, I know God had me there to protect my baby daughter from demons taking over her body. I had never seen anything like this except in the movie the *The Exorcist.*

Dianna also had a brain aneurysm that required brain surgery. I asked the doctor why this happened to my daughter, and he told me that this was all caused from smoking. He also told me that she would probably have lots of seizures and would probably die from that.

Again, prayer was my only resource. It was all up to God. Only He holds her future!

Dianna had extensive physical therapy for months. She was paralyzed on the left side. She could no longer sing and perform the way she once did.

Dianna hated the way her body had betrayed her. She took her anger out on her family, especially her mother and people who were like she had become. The rudeness I saw in my daughter was evil. Again, all I could do was to pray for her.

God gifted our daughter with a voice that no one in our family had. She was one of the most talented people I had ever seen or heard.

When she began singing, I traveled everywhere with her to all of her shows. Then she realized that there was lots of money to be made at the bars. She then began booking her own shows and leaving Momma behind.

I watched her go from a very beautiful, kind, and talented young woman to a woman who lots of men wanted. I hated seeing what was happening to her, but she refused to listen to me when I tried to speak to her about it.

She began smoking and drinking to extreme. She used smoking as a way to calm her nerves. Before she started singing in bars, she never had nerves that needed calming.

I knew the enemy wouldn't be attacking her if something very valuable wasn't inside her. Thieves don't break into an empty house. I knew she had a divine purpose!

CHAPTER XIII

Life Goes On

I did all I knew to do for Dianna, but it just wasn't enough. She had been so independent for so long that she didn't want to give into her momma helping her.

Dianna had just bought a new house before she had the stroke. Her best friend told me that Dianna would probably want to sell it, but that was not to be.

Dianna had been dating Jeff before the stroke and she thought he was going to marry her, but during her stay in the rehab, he took the ring off her finger and he disappeared.

She didn't see him for a very long time. One day, I was taking her to Fort Worth for therapy when I saw Jeff driving next to us on I-20. I said, "Oh, look. There's Jeff." After I said that, I wished I hadn't because she didn't see him until I mentioned that he was there.

After that, she made every effort to contact him against my better judgment. She finally got him to answer the phone and they talked for quite a long time. It wasn't too long until Dianna talked Gino, one of her friends, into moving her out of her parent's home and into her own home.

Shortly after that, Dianna and Jeff married. I'm sure she thought he would pay her bills and care for her, but that wasn't the case. Jeff began abusing Dianna both physically and mentally.

Dianna would call the police to protect herself. When they got to her house, Jeff would tell them that Dianna was abusing him. Then they would both be hauled off.

One time, I was in Amarillo when I got a phone call from Dianna telling me she was in jail and needed her medicine. There was nothing I could do to help her, I was five hours away.

Her daughter Courtney came to help. When she arrived, she only had enough money to get one of them out of jail. Courtney chose to get Jeff out of jail thinking he would get Dianna's medicine to her and get her released.

Dianna finally got out of jail and went back to Jeff. He only abused her more. She called me and her Daddy to listen on her phone one evening when Jeff was screaming profanities at her. Every other word started with "F."

Her father and I went straight to her house and made Jeff leave. They soon got divorced.

Dianna had a cousin in Denton who owned a large home that Dianna could share. They lived together for about two years. Dianna seemed to get better while with her cousin. At the same time, Dianna began going to a church in South Lake, Texas by the name of Gateway.

I almost used the word coincidence again, but now I know that everything is a divine appointment. Nothing is coincidence! During the time Dianna lived with her cousin, I was planning to build a reception hall to have weddings at the Praise Pavilion. The only problem was that the economy was flat lining at the time.

We barely made enough money to keep our office open. I had to refinance properties in order to pay bills. Building a reception hall was slowly becoming nearly impossible.

I would quite often go to the Praise Pavilion to pray and be alone with the Lord. About four years had passed since Glenn and Harold built the pavilion. By now it was 2012.

I was getting so discouraged about not having money to build with that I began shouting at the Lord, "Please just give me a sign that You want a church, You provide the money and the builders and I will build it." Harold had built a mailbox in the shape of a little house. It held the wedding brochures.

I just said to God, "Let someone put money in that box as proof you want a church and I will build it!" I stomped up to the box and pulled the lid open and there was a five dollar bill! No one had ever put any money in that box and now when I asked God to prove it to me, there it was!

I took the money and ran all around the gazebos and praised God for giving me proof. I drove back to my office and ran inside to show Glenn that God had given me proof that He wanted a church on this property. Glenn said, "If God gave you the proof, He will provide."

CHAPTER XIV

Miracle after Miracle

That was about one thirty in the afternoon. Glenn had a friend come into our office and ask Glenn to go look at a piece of equipment to sell. It was past lunch and I was getting hungry. I decided to go across the highway to the new Subway and get a pizza.

My grandson, Dawson and Scott Wimberly came in about that time and they also wanted pizza. We got our pizza, ate most of it, and had to return to the office. Levi, Dawson's brother, came into the Subway just as we were leaving. Dawson decided to stay with his brother.

Scott and I were traveling back to the office. As we approached the bridge crossing I-20, a speeding car came from the interstate. There was no way I could get away from her hitting my car.

I sped up to keep her from hitting me broadside. She hit the back of my car, making it spin around, and then she hit the front of my car, totaling it. Some people who came upon the wreck called the ambulance to take me to the hospital.

I had a broken left arm and a concussion. When the doctor told me that I tried to make a joke of it, saying, "So what's new? That's what I had a year and two days ago, when I fell on the ice."

The doctor told me to go to my primary care physician in three days. I said, "No way, she wouldn't sign off on my AFLAC insurance." She said, "She didn't believe in AFLAC."

I told her I didn't care if she believed in it or not, I did and I needed her to sign or I wouldn't get paid for the accident. She never signed the paperwork and I never got paid.

I was so ill from the concussion that I couldn't argue with her about it. The year passed as I went from being completely disoriented to finally getting back to normal, when the second accident happened.

I have since learned not to argue with God when he says no. Just wait on the Lord. When the second accident happened and the doctor told me to go see my primary physician, I told him, "No, I wouldn't go see her, because she wouldn't sign my paperwork." I asked him to give me another list of doctors and I would choose another one. As he turned to get a list, I prayed a very short prayer, "Lord, guide me."

When he returned with the list, I just pointed to the list and picked Dr. Melcher. In three days, I visited Dr. Melcher. When he came into the exam room, I immediately asked, "Do you believe in AFLAC?" He answered, "Yes, and I tell anyone who asked to get on it."

I told him what had happened the year before and he said, "If you will get your paperwork from the hospital, I will sign off on it and this accident and get you paid for both."

I got the paperwork and Dr. Melcher signed for the accident in 2011 and the car accident in 2012. About two weeks later, I had

$35,000.00 in my hands. That was enough money to buy all the framing wood for our church.

Just before the accident, I had another miracle happen. There was a small two-story house at the Praise Pavilion in the spot that I wanted to build on. I was showing Glenn the spot where I wanted to move the house. I wanted it next door to my house.

As Glenn and I were talking about the location I wanted, he told me, "No, you can't put the house in this location. I asked, "Why?" He said, "Look up, you can't put a house under power lines."

I said, "Why don't we just ask the power company to move them for us?" Glenn said, "That would cost a fortune." I hadn't noticed the power lines before he said that. I just said, okay and I looked up and said to the Lord, "I want those power lines moved."

The next morning, I had just gotten to my office when I heard the bell on our front door. A man in a blue Tri-County shirt asked, "Who owns this property?" The lady at our reception desk answered and said, "Ms. Littlepage, she is in her office."

The man walked into my office and asked me if I would do him a favor. I answered, "Yes, sir, if I can." He asked if I would allow him to move the power lines on my property. I sat there for a few seconds in amazement. Then I said, "Sure, I would do that favor for you."

Glenn and Harold hadn't finished building the third gazebo at that time. They were working on it when they noticed that the power line was right up against the roof of the last gazebo. The day that the power company moved the line off our property, they were beginning to build the roof.

I went to the Praise Pavilion to see the progress of the power company when I noticed the power line was against the roof of the gazebo. I asked the lineman if he would allow me to keep the power pole and would he please move it twenty feet to the north so that I could use it for a security light pole. He said yes, he sure would let us keep it and he would move it for us.

I went to town for about an hour and when I came back, he was installing the pole where I ask him to put it. I thought this is a perfect time to ask how much it would have cost if I had to pay to move the power lines. He said, "Oh my, that last time we moved a power line, it was three million dollars and this time it is five times that much and an oil company is paying for it. I just looked up and said, "Thank you. I knew I was *your* favorite kid."

We had a visitor come to our office one day. He had just come in to visit a little while. This was several months after I had the bad fall on the ice. I recognized him, but I couldn't remember his name. When I got the opportunity, I said, "I know you but I can't think of your name." He turned to me and said, "Well, Barbara, I'm Coy Carter. I used to be Parker County sheriff." As he told me his name, I heard the Lord tell me to ask him about a man with a barn full of lumber. I thought, *Lord that's not real holy, but I believe You speak to me. I will ask him.* I said, "Coy, do you know a man with a barn full of lumber?" Without skipping a beat, Coy answered, "Yes, I do. He's over the Brock Bridge and in front of the elementary school. There's a red brick house with a barn behind it and it's full of lumber."

I told Glenn to take Coy and go check that barn. They left and Glenn called me in about five minutes and said, "You won't believe what I'm looking at." I said, "A barn full of lumber?" He said, "Yes." I asked him how much the man wanted and he told me $2,500—the exact amount of money I had saved for the church.

The miracles just kept on coming. One day, David called and asked if he could rent the two-story house from me. I said, "Yes, you sure can and I won't charge you what I do everyone else." He said, "Great, and I can pay you for a full year?" I ordered the chairs for our church thinking when David pays me, I will have enough money to pay for the chairs.

The day the chairs were due in, I got another phone call from David. He said, "Momma, Sabrina doesn't want that house and I can't rent it from you." He said, "I know I promised, and I feel bad, but she just won't move into it." I said, "Don't worry, David. You are not my source, God is, and He won't let me down." That day, I went to the mail box and brought the mail in.

I found a letter from Fidelity, a company that pays two very small retirement checks to Glenn each month. I started to hand him the letter, but I decided I better open it myself.

When I opened it, there was a check in the amount of $5,000. Wow, we never got a check from that company like that before. The chairs were $4,800. I called the chair company and told them I would be there that day to get the chairs.

One day, Glenn and I went to Crowley, Texas to bring Melody, our great granddaughter, back for a visit. On the way, Melody asks if we could eat at Luby's. That was one of her favorite places to eat on the way to visit Na-Na and Da-Da's. We were eating when my phone rang.

It was Tim's daughter. She said, "Ms. Barbara, Daddy is in a coma and no one can wake him. Please come." I told Melody and Glenn to finish eating because Tim was unconscious and we were needed.

I had been praying that I could do miracles like Jesus did, but I'm sure I didn't think I would ever have His powers. All the way to the hospital, I prayed that I could wake Tim when no one else had been able.

When we got to the hospital, I ask God to give me the ability to lay hands on Tim and wake him. As I approached Tim's room, his daughter was standing out by the door. She said, "Daddy is still unconscious."

I walked in and laid my hand on his arm and said in a calming voice, "Tim, it's time to wake up." Suddenly, he opened his eyes and said, "Damn, I have overslept." He thought I was waking him to go to work. He was released from the hospital that day. He never had any more incidents like that.

Tim was another miracle that God gave me. One day, I had a rent house that needed remodeling. I hired a man to do the job. He found Tim an excellent carpenter to do the work for him. I came to inspect the house and found the man I hired lying on the floor asleep. Tim was there working as he was supposed to.

I asked Tim if he could finish the job by himself and how long would it take. He said, "I can have this job finished in a week. I fired the first man and hired Timothy.

Tim told me later that his real name was Tim on his birth certificate, but for some reason, I couldn't call him that, I kept calling him Timothy.

After a short time, I figured out why I couldn't call him Tim. I had a renter who always paid his rent on time, but one day he came into my office and said he couldn't pay rent that month. I asked him why, he said, because he had just been laid off from his job.

I asked him what he did for a living. He said, "I build cabinets and doors." His name was Paul. When I first made the vow to build a church, I told God if He would provide the money and builders, I would make sure we had a church on the property.

God provided the money and the builders—Timothy and Paul!

Another time after dark, I left the house to walk out to the office. I usually wear flip flops and short pants, although we have seen copperheads and rattlesnakes on our parking lot. I tried to watch out for any snakes.

As I was walking toward the office, I noticed a copperhead lying on the ground about six or eight inches from my foot. I froze in place so as to not attack attention of the snake.

I had my cell phone in my pocket so I called Glenn to tell him to grab a stick with a nail in it to come kill the snake. The first miracle was that we had a stick with a nail leaning in the corner of the living room. Tim had needed it to reach something that was too high for him to reach and he forgot to take it out to the shop.

The second miracle was that I decided to speak to the snake and command it to leave and not bite me. I said, "In the name of Jesus, you turn and leave me and don't try to bite me." The snake turned and started to craw away when Glenn came out and hit it with the nail and killed it. Again, all I could say was "Thank you, Lord."

CHAPTER XV

Testing Time

At the time I decided to listen to the Lord and build the church, I only had a few tests. When my parents and my grandmother died, I thought that was a real test. It wasn't until Dianna had the stroke and aneurism that I started really having to trust God. That's when I said, "God, she is Yours, You take care of her."

Before that, I always felt like my family was safe from the evils of this world. I had three perfect children, seven grandchildren, and two great grandchildren. We had escaped mental retardation and every other source of pain that touches some other families—at least I made myself believe that.

Before Dianna had the stroke, her daughter Caitlin started having hearing problems. We couldn't understand why all of a sudden she couldn't hear. Dianna took her to the doctor and found out that Caitlin had Alport Syndrome. This is a disease mostly boys get. Nobody knows for sure how they get the syndrome, but it is thought that the gene is passed on to the child from the mother's side.

"Alport syndrome is a form of inherited nephritis (inflammation of the kidneys), typically developing at a young age, mostly in males.

The disorder causes progressive deterioration of parts of the kidney and gradual reduction in kidney function. Some types of Alport Syndrome may also affect hearing and vision."

As time went on, Caitlin required a kidney transplant. Her father, Clint White, was a match for Caitlin. Caitlin was told that she would probably be in her forties or fifties before that would be needed, but she had to have the transplant when she was twenty-three. Again, I found myself in constant prayer. I couldn't do anything for her. Every time I thought of her, I said, "Lord she's Yours, and please take care of her." I was used to taking care of my children and now the only way I could care for her was to pray.

I couldn't imagine what else the devil would throw at me, but I soon found out. In the spring of 2014 Timothy, the man who the Lord sent to build our church, was cleaning out our pool. He decided to empty the water so that he could repair the cracks and repaint the pool. I told him he had better get it done quickly because I heard it was supposed to start raining. I had been told that a pool would float out of the ground if the water was out of it and it rained.

Timothy told me not to worry, he would get it done before it started raining. By the time he drained the pool, it started raining before he could do any repairs. He thought it probably wouldn't rain for too long and he could just refill the pool. But it didn't stop raining. It rained for forty days and forty nights. The only other time I heard of it raining forty days and nights was when Noah built the arc.

I watched as the pool lowly rose out of the ground. I was told our pool was the largest home pool in Parker County. It was fifty-five thousand gallons and twelve feet on the deep end.

Since we built the church, we had been using the swimming pool for baptisms. There was nothing anyone could do, but watch it rise. We had to hire a man with a bulldozer to come and completely demolish our pool at a cost of $8,000.

While that was happening, every Sunday as I would be giving my message, I would look at the south wall in our church and see cracks every four feet as the wall dropped about three inches. The rains had flooded underneath the church and I had no idea that this was happening until it was too late to do anything about it. All I could do was to pray that the wall didn't fall down.

We have oak floors and the water under the foundation was causing the oak boards to buckle. Timothy would go to the church every week and repair floor boards to keep people from tripping over the boards.

Finally, one day, I told Timothy that the floor in the bride's room was soft and he needed to take it out so that we could see what was going on under the church. When he took the floor out, there was a river running under the church.

I called a foundation company out of Dallas to come make the repairs. They gave me a bid of $9,000 and told me I didn't need to pay them until the job was done. I signed a contract and they started the job. The first week they wanted me to pay them $4,000 to cover their employees pay. I objected, but paid what they asked.

The next week they ask for another $3,000. Again I objected, but paid it. This went on until the job was nearly finished and by that time I had paid $25,000 for the floor to be repaired. I was quickly running out of money and told them they needed to finish and leave.

They didn't finish the job and asked for more money and I refused to pay so they ended up by putting a judgment on the church, and both my husband and me. Again, all I could do at this point was to pray. God, You will have to finish this job, I can't afford any more.

Timothy and Glenn went into the ladies' restroom and finished the job. They had to haul dirt out from under the floor and then put in new treated lumber and replace the flooring. They got this done within a couple of weeks, at a cost of the lumber only.

While we were dealing with the church floor, I was diagnosed with breast cancer in January of 2016. I waited two full months before starting chemo. I decided to take an Indian medicine called MUD. After about two months, I had people from church and family members beg me to take chemo to stay alive and healthy.

I took two chemo treatments and the lump that was there before was gone. I had been praying that God would heal me. I told the doctors that I didn't have cancer and I was going to stop taking the chemo treatments.

They were appalled that I would stop because they thought that the cancer was still there. They finally decided to do a mammogram and sonogram to check if there was cancer. The test revealed that there was no cancer. They couldn't believe what they were seeing.

I knew God had healed me. While suffering with the chemo treatments, I cried out to the Lord to help me and He did! I told Him I knew what I was suffering was nothing compared to what He suffered and if it was His will, I would do whatever He wanted to do. I lost my hair and the pain was unbearable at times, but with God's help I got through it.

While taking the chemo, one of my friends called to ask if I was okay. I replied, "Yes, why are you asking?" My friend said she was looking at Facebook and saw where Dianna had posted a DNA test showing that Glenn was not her father. She said according to what she could tell, it did not say he was not her father. I sat there in amazement that Dianna would do something like that to hurt not only me, but her father.

Dianna had convinced her brother David to take a DNA test to prove that they were not full siblings. David thought about it and decided to take the test. I'm sure to prove that he was her full brother.

When the test came back, the person who gave them the results made a mistake and told them that they "were not full siblings." Of course they believed what the devil wanted them to believe. I'm sure they were both very hurt by this news.

Dianna posted it on Facebook and David brought the results to my office. Both Glenn and I were gone at the time so David gave the results to our office girl and told her that he and Dianna were not full siblings.

When Glenn and I arrived she gave us the paperwork and told us what David had said. Glenn and I were appalled that this was happening to us, especially since I was in the process of taking chemo. I immediately called the DNA clinic and asked why they would lie to my children. The man who answered the phone was extremely rude to me because he believed what he had told my children was the truth.

When I asked why he would tell them that he said, "I don't have a dog in the hunt." I said back to him, "I don't care about dogs, I want this corrected." I told him I would be there in thirty minutes to get this fixed.

When we got there, I asked again why. Again, he answered with the dog comment. I tried not to cry, but I just couldn't believe he was so cavalier about this. As I began to cry, Glenn spoke up and said, "Well, I'm here and you can take my DNA and prove that I am Dianna's father."

So Glenn provided his DNA for the proof. The man wrapped it in a Fed Ex package and said he would get it off the next day. I told him "No, I will take it right now and send it in."

The next morning at about eight, I received a phone call from the DNA office from a woman who was nearly shouting to me that they had made a terrible mistake. This was before the Fed Ex package had been received for revised testing. The man who didn't have a dog in the hunt made a terrible mistake! I don't blame him; I blame the devil who was trying to tear up my family, my ministry, and me.

The floors continued to give us trouble for the next two years. The oak boards would buckle and Timothy would repair them as needed, until one day he decided to cut a hole in the middle of the church. It was about twenty square feet.

About October 2016, we had a huge hole in the middle of the church. This time Timothy, David, and Glenn dug dirt out until they got it low enough to crawl under and remove the old rotted lumber and replace it with new treated lumber. This time it only cost the price of the lumber. My prayer was answered. The church is back in great condition.

I started to write this book because David, my son, told me to tell my story if I wanted to build a new church. I had told him I didn't want to borrow money to build because I knew that God told me to build the first building and He provided the money. This time, I just couldn't see how enough money for a building like I wanted could come in. That's when David said, "Momma, if you tell your story people will buy the book."

I have told things in this book that were kept secret for over fifty years. I never wanted to hurt anyone by telling the stories, but I thought if I told them they might help someone else who feels they are not worthy to serve God. After I built the church for two years, I kept praying that God would send someone to bring the message because I didn't feel worthy.

I have learned through writing this book that there are no such things as coincidence, everything is divine appointments. Fifty years after my graduation, I ran into Mike, not intentionally. I believe now it was a divine appointment. I needed someone who really knew me to tell me that I was chosen by God and I needed to believe in myself. Mike told me that if God would use Paul, He would certainly use Barbara!

I know that marrying Glenn was not my idea, but I know without Glenn I wouldn't be the person I am today. Glenn has always been by my side and he believed in me before I believed in myself. So for that, I thank you Glenn and forgive you for anything that I have held against you for all these years. I wrote this book with the belief that the devil will keep you in bondage if you don't face him head-on. I don't want anyone to beat Glenn down for an immature judgment he made at an early age. He is a Godly man and I love him.

In writing my story, I learned how quickly things turn around when you forgive someone who has hurt you. I know you love me and I love you. I have prayed for years that you were the man I needed and by writing this book I know that you are the man I needed. God allowed you to come into my life. There are no coincidences!

My three children have learned to trust him. We're still praying for the grandchildren and great grandchildren, but we know they are God's kids!

FOCUS: Psalm 63:1 says, "O God, You are my God; It seems redundant, unless you understand how easily WE ARE DISTRACTED, how easily we ALLOW OTHER THINGS to TAKE HIS place in our lives. NEVER let it be! DON'T ALLOW IT! With deepest longing I WILL SEEK YOU; My soul [my life, my very self] THIRSTS for You, MY FLESH LONGS for & SIGHS for You, in a DRY & WEARY LAND where NO water is." NOTHING BUT GOD CAN SATISFY you. SPEND QUALITY TIME with HIM EVERY DAY. T/R/U/S/T Him."

CHAPTER XVI

Revelations

Just as I was finishing this book, the devil tried our family even more. Leighton Shifflett, the twenty-four-year-old son of Stacy Riley was found dead in bed on the morning of January 18, 2017. For the first time, David was facing the responsibility of caring for a loved one who was in pain over the loss of her precious son.

David called me after Leighton passed away. He was again in such pain. The kind of pain that makes me want to hold him. He said to me, "Momma, I know now why God allowed my wife to leave me like she did. Stacy helped me through that and now I'm here to help her through this."

Life does not prepare anyone for a journey like that. At one time, I had commented that our family was so blessed that we had never had to deal with any illness or death of a loved one. Be very careful what you say, because the devil can hear your words. Just when you think you've got the world by the tail, he will do whatever it takes to bring you down and get your mind off of our Lord and Savior Jesus Christ.

I was preparing to baptize a woman in our church when these scriptures came to my attention.

"But he said to me, 'My grace is sufficient for you, for my power is made perfect in weakness.' Therefore, I will boast all the more gladly about my weaknesses, so that Christ's power may rest on me" (2 Corinthians 12:9).

"And we know that in all things God works for the good of those who love him, who have been called according to his purpose" (Romans 8:28).

I remember telling my daughter Dianna that all things work the for good of those who love the Lord and are called according to His purpose on the day that the pastor with whom she loved dearly uninvited her to sing at "Baby in Bethlehem."

Dianna had just divorced for the third time and the pastor thought it was a bad example for her to sing after that. As I look back on that, I realize that was the devil trying to discourage Dianna from serving God.

After the pastor really thought about what damage he was doing to Dianna and the family, he decided to allow her to sing, although at the very end of the service, which by that time, most of the people were gone. She did sing and she did it as unto the Lord and I couldn't have been prouder of her. As I sat there watching her with tears running down her face, I knew that she was doing it for the right reason. I was witnessing the scripture come to life 'My grace is sufficient for you, for my power is made perfect in weakness.' Therefore, I will boast all the more gladly about my weaknesses, so that Christ's power may rest on me."

Our family is living proof that God has each of us in the palm of His hand and He will not put more on us than we can bear.

"The concept that God will not put more on us than we can bear does have biblical support as long as one keeps in mind the needed balance between what God sovereignly allows according to His wisdom and purpose(s)and our human responsibility to trust and draw near to Him."

1 Corinthians 10:13 "No trial has overtaken you that is not faced by others. And God is faithful: He will not let you be tried beyond what you are able to bear, but with the trial will also provide a way out so that you may be able to endure it."

"When thou passest through the waters, I will be with thee; and through the rivers, they shall not overflow thee: when thou walkest through the fire, thou shalt not be burned; neither shall the flame kindle upon thee." Isaiah 43:2-3 KJV

As I was preparing to end this book, I was resting on a Monday morning. After the funeral of Leighton, visiting loved ones in hospice, and having our first in-church baptism, I was very exhausted. As I lay in my bed, the phone rang. It was Glenn asking me to come to the office to help with a U-haul customer.

When I got to the office, I recognized the man as Wade Harvey, someone with whom I had worked before. As we were finishing his contract, I began telling him about this book and how it got started. I told him about all the butterflies and how I had never seen that many before.

He told me that he is a truck driver and every year at that time of year, his truck radiator would be covered with butterflies. He also told me about them migrating once a year. As I listened to Wade tell me about the migration, I began to have chills on my arms. When I told him about my chills, he too, rubbed his arms with chills. I originally thought that God was showing me how He loved us and what we were discussing was being blessed by Him and when I began waiting on the Lord and asking Him for confirmation about what I thought He was telling me to do.

This seemed like confirmation long before I learned of the Monarch butterflies migrating once a year.

I decided after Wade left to investigate and this is what I learned.

"Monarch butterflies (*Danaus plexippus*) perform annual migrations across North America which has been called "one of the most spectacular natural phenomena in the world".[1]

Starting in September and October, eastern/northeastern populations migrate from southern Canada and the United States to overwintering sites in central Mexico where they arrive around November."

I am so amazed that God loves us so much that He would let us witness one of the most spectacular natural phenomena in the world to validate what we want to do with the church.

CHAPTER XVII

What is Grief and How Does It Feel

This is another miracle that happened to cause me to believe that God had truly chosen me to build the church. I wrote this article to appear on my Praise Pavilion.org website. The Fountain of Tears was delivered unfinished. When the lady who was hired to stain the statue began to spray, the wind picked up to about 80 mph from no wind at all. Glenn begged her to stop and please don't spray because the stain would streak across her body. That didn't happen, but as you can see, the only streaks were on her face, showing how grief really hurts.

> What is grief and how does it feel
> The look on Mary's face tells.
> "The Fountain of Tears"

The Fountain of Tears is a fountain that was donated to the Praise Pavilion by "A Hole in My Heart Ministry." The Fountain of Tears was the vision of Autumn Ater after the death of her son, Robert. Robert was born with multiple birth defects and ultimately passed away when he was fourteen years old.

After Robert's death, Autumn's grief almost overtook her. That is, until God gave her the vision to have a fountain built in honor of her precious son. Autumn planned how the fountain would look and where she could display the fountain. She wanted to share the fountain with other bereaved parents. For three years, Autumn had fundraisers and donations to build the fountain. At last, in March of 2011, the fountain was complete. Autumn contacted every public park in Parker County, Texas but to no avail. No one would allow her to put the fountain on display. It seems that an atheist had forced the county to not display Christ-like images in the public places. That's when Autumn contacted Barbara Littlepage.

Autumn had known Barbara from her college years and heard that Barbara had a memorial park in memory of her parents. When Autumn contacted Barbara, there was an instant renewal of friendship and a kindred spirit. Another factor that seemed God-like was that Barbara had dreamed of having a fountain in the gardens for the last three years. There was no hesitation the fountain had found a home.

On April 11, 2011 (which was Barbara and Glenn's forty-seventh wedding anniversary), the fountain was delivered. Seems God validates everything that is done in His name. This was definitely a sign from God. The unveiling ceremony took place on April 23, 2011.

We thought how great, God has shown us favor by this sign—that is, until the fountain was stained. We couldn't believe our eyes when the stain was sprayed on the fountain. The wind was blowing at least eighty miles per hour. We were worried that it might streak across the fountain. The stain not only did not streak across the statue, it streaked down the cheeks like tears. The pain of losing a child was instantly manifested in Mary's face. Glenn Littlepage witnessed this happening.

The Catholic Church was contacted immediately to verify that this was not man made, but God had indeed given us another sign of His pleasure in what we were doing.

The Praise Pavilion

The Praise Pavilion was established to honor our parents after the death of Barbara Littlepage's father, W. A. Phillips in January 2006 followed by her mother's death in 2007. The rock garden has the Ten Commandments with a beautiful rock waterfall that runs three ways around the Commandments. This symbolizes the Trinity.

There are three grand pavilions again symbolizing the Trinity, which begun being called the "Praise Pavilion" because Barbara Littlepage would lift her hands in praise to the Lord for allowing them to honor their parents with such beautiful gardens. Money has always been an issue, but somehow God provided. We are very thankful for any donations that are made to help us continue to share this with the public.

The Ten Commandments

The Ten Commandments was another miracle God gave me to see that I was truly in His will. I decided to search for stones to make the Ten Commandments. The day I started the search, I got into my car and decided to pray before I left the parking lot. I sat at the driveway entrance for serveral minutes before I would leave. I didn't know for sure which way to turn. When I felt the Holy Spirit move me to turn to the right, then I drove away, not knowing where I was going.

I drove until I felt the unction to turn again to the right. Then I came to a blinking light where I waited again for the Holy Spirit to move me. I again turned, but this time to the left. I drove serveral miles until I felt the move to turn into a business that was owned by one of Glenn's cousins. I walked into the Richard's Sign Company in Mineral Wells, Texas and met Russell Richards for the first time, the husband of Glenn's cousin.

I told him what I was looking for and he told me to look at the back of his building because he had some stones. I looked and came back to tell him nothing would work. He then told me to go way back behind the tall trees and brush because some new stones were back there. Again, I was wearing flip flops and short pants. Since this is snake country, I was extra cautious to watch out for snakes. As I cleared the weeds and trees, I saw a light, like an angel was shining over these two stones. I know God lead me to them. There was no other way I could have found them so quickly.

These are pictures of Barbara and Mike in 1963, 1964 and fifty years later.

Barbara and Mike 6/20/2014

Mike and Barbara

Mike and Brabara 1964 Chevy

We had no pictures before the wedding. I was determined to smile and look very happy in each one.

Barbara and Glenn 1st Photo

Barbara and Glenn 2014

Barbara and Glenn(April 11, 1964)

Barbara and Glenn 50 years later

These are pictures of Dianna before and after the stroke.

Dianna 2007   Dianna 7/31/2008

These are pictures of my little sister Patty before and after AIDS.

Patty as a child

Three days before she passed away

These are the Littlepage cousins and a picture of Glenn at age nine.

Littlepage Cousins

Glenn Age 9

Pictures of Daddy's family and his 80th birthday cake with Momma

Daddy's 80th Birthday

Daddy's 80th cake

Picture of Dianna, David and Matt. Picture of Daddy, momma, grandma and Glenn and me and our kids.

Dianna, David Matt and Family

This is the jeep that daddy built for his girls about 1958

Trying to be brave when my hair started falling out.

First day hair came out

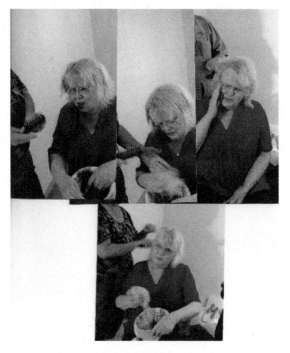

The day my hair came out

Here are some more pictures of my granddaughter, Courtney shaving my head. The next group is of me having lots of pain after chemo. The third group is me trying to make peace with a bald head. The fourth group is when my hair came out for the first time

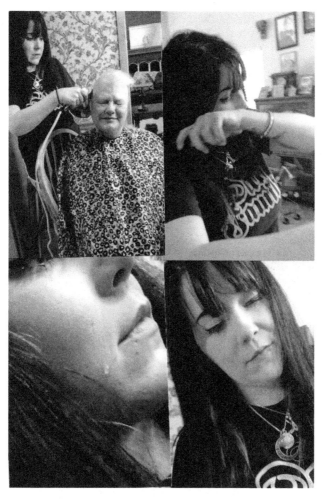

Courtney shaving my head

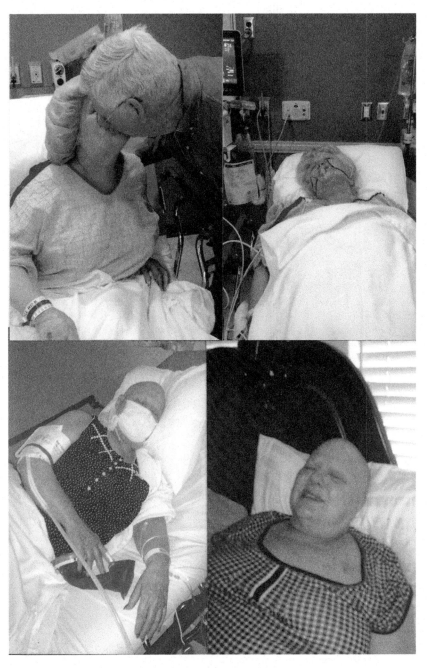

Pain of Chemo

Courtney, Caitlin and Glenn shaving my head
and I holding the little girl named Hazey.

Courtney and Caitlyn trying on wig after my head was shaved.
Making peace with bald head

It's of Mike, Melody (our great granddaughter)
Me, and Glenn at our fiftieth class reunion.

About the Author

I was a typical '60s girl, bought up with the Christian faith of my parents. I was fun-loving, but very serious about my faith and commitment to love the Lord and be a good girl. I was popular and had lots of friends, both male and female.

I loved school although I wasn't too concerned about my grades. I did pass all my classes, but studying was low on my priority list. I loved going to parties, swimming, having sleepovers with girlfriends and going to the walk-in movie. I had friends visit quite often.

Our house was on the main street in Arlington, Texas and every time one of my friends would drive past my house, they would honk. I would run to look out my front bedroom window and be delighted that someone honked.

I worked at the local Grants Department store to earn my spending money. Momma and Daddy were very strict about my curfew. It was 10:00 p.m. I always made it. I was an obedient daughter.

My life was as normal as I could make it after I married Glenn. We had three wonderful babies and our lives were well ordered. I tried very hard to be the best wife I could be. Glenn had the idea that his wife wouldn't work, but extra money was needed, so I stayed home and cared for other women's babies while they worked.

After twenty-five years of marriage and after taking college classes I told Glenn that unless he allowed me to make most of the decisions about our income and become more involved with whatever business we got into I would not stay with him.

He gave in to me and agreed that I could make more of the decisions. That's when our trucking business was started. I established all the assumed name paperwork, printed business cards, got signs for our trucks, began contacting customers and thus began Littlepage Logistics, Inc.

We had a very successful trucking company for twenty-five years, then Daddy and momma became very ill and I spent all my time caring for them. After they passed away our daughter was stricken with a stroke and an aneurism. Later I was diagnosed with cancer.

I didn't know how our future would ever get back to normal, but by God's grace our lives have gotten back on track. I told the Lord I was finished trying to take care of everybody and make sure we all looked normal to the world. He had to take charge and HE did!!

Now my passion is our church. I put God first in my life and he has allowed me to built a church and become the pastor. I used to fret over my children and I was constantly concerned about our income in our old age, but the Lord has that well in hand.

CPSIA information can be obtained
at www.ICGtesting.com
Printed in the USA
FSOW04n2330171117
41252FS